WITHDRAWN

Other Books by Margaret Halsey

WITH MALICE TOWARD SOME
SOME OF MY BEST FRIENDS ARE SOLDIERS
COLOR BLIND

The Folks
at Home

by

MARGARET HALSEY

19 · 52

SIMON AND SCHUSTER

To My Father

A Man of Character

TABLE OF CONTENTS

———

vii

The Folks at Home

I

The Upward Step

———

EXCEPT FOR the circumstance that I am now entering my fifth decade of it, I have no particular qualifications for writing about American life. But aside from being a female, I have no particular qualifications for being a mother, either. I am, however, the parent of a four-year-old daughter; and this book is, in a manner of speaking, some thinking out loud I am doing in her behalf. The American society—through its newspapers, picture magazines, movies, comics and radio-television—is soon going to move in on my little girl. She will very shortly be old enough to ask naïve and devastating questions about the behavior of the tense and anxious grownups. When that time comes, I should like to be prepared with a few unhurried and non-evasive answers.

By profounder thinkers than I, it has been noted that

there are certain widely accepted and pretty much unquestioned beliefs—notably about money—on which most of American living is based. It occurs to her father and me that instead of buying our daughter the customary television set, we might (in terms of her whole life) perform an equally benevolent service by taking hold of some of these beliefs and giving them a quick flap, to see whether any moths fly out. If a cat may look at a king, certainly a parent may look at an entrepreneur.

What is the real nature of American life? The query may not be as complex as it seems at first. The pressures and tensions—admitted even by the advertisements to be characteristic of American living—are universal. That is to say, they operate with splendid impartiality on "haves" and "have-nots," talented and untalented, conservative and liberal, minority and majority, management and labor, Democrat and Republican. This harsh democracy of tension would seem to imply that there is some kind of least common denominator which is producing it. If such a least common denominator exists, the people who most need to know about it are the parents of small and growing children.

I am forty-two years of age and my daughter is four, which probably makes me the Oldest Living Mother of a Small Child. Since a rather longer interval than is customary intervened between my birth and my daughter's, I am perhaps more conscious than other mothers of four-year-olds of how times have changed. Like many of my contemporaries, I grew up in the long, cold shadow of

2

Victorian dutifulness. This kind of upbringing was not without its advantages. In its way, it prepared people to accept responsibility. But customs and conventions are perpetually evolving and developing; and in our enlightened age, it is generally agreed that children need love.

Now that I have a daughter of my own, I am glad the emphasis in child care has switched from demanding obedience to giving affection. It seems to me to represent a large step forward in man's upward struggle toward the stars. We now have permission to love our children, as even fairly recent vintages of parents did not. But it does not seem to be enough. I think most parents would agree that bringing up children in the present-day United States is both a tentative and a taxing job. Indeed, the enormous American literature on child care is mute evidence that most American parents do not function parentally with easy and joyous self-confidence.

The books on child care, however, usually concentrate solely on the children. They rather take for granted the country in which the children are living. The following chapters grew up out of a notion that perhaps some kind of interpretation of the American scene could be made which would bring the task of raising children into somewhat clearer focus. For those of my readers who have no children, or whose children are ravaged old characters of twenty-five, the interpretation of American life which ensues will provide either the pleasurable feeling of recognition or the possibly even more pleasurable feeling of

3

discovering a human being who is completely and utterly in the wrong.

Until I was thirty-eight, all I knew about parenthood was what one could pick up from having had two of them. To be sure, during a period of temporary affluence, I did what so many affluent Americans do—laid my dreams and my childhood (my version of it) in the archepiscopal laps of a couple of classical Freudian analyists. In the beginning of these experiences, I was entranced by the delightfully heart-rending picture of sensitive, appealing little me being trodden all over by brutal, Oedipal giants. But when at long last it began to dawn on me—celerity on the pick-up is not one of my strong points—that the giants had themselves once been children in the slightly untender atmosphere of the American nineteenth century, the magic went out of it. Freud's hot little vacuum of parent and child was not for me.

This is not to say that I do not contemplate with reverence and awe the courage and the sovereign intellect of Sigmund Freud. There are few Americans or Western Europeans who do not owe something to that unbowed head. But one swallow does not make a summer; and one man does not make a science. I was trained—conscientiously trained—for a life that World War I extinguished four years after I was born; and I have spent most of my adult years trying to keep my footing among a long series of unheralded novelties. I have been able to get a certain amount of scientific help in this balancing act, but it has come from the relatively inexpensive method of reading

4

here and there among the published works of the many—
and sometimes acidly divergent—scientists who picked up
and branched out from where Freud left off. It was not,
however, until four years ago, when I achieved a child of
my own, that I began to see that this unnerving gap between childhood and adult life was not as peculiar to me
as I had thought it was. It happens to all Americans. It is
going to happen to my little girl, unless her father and I
can think of something to do about it.

Since I have been a parent, I have noticed that there
are two major particulars in which my daughter's early
life has no kinship whatsoever with my early years. One
of these particulars lies in the circumstance that when I
and my contemporaries were four years old, it was not
possible to make very much money out of children. There
were no comic books, no radio, no television, and the
movies were still in a fledgling state. Except for oatmeal
and library books, children were not consumers. Today,
however, her father and I are by no means the only people who love our daughter. Almost literally, she is worth
her weight in gold to private enterprise. Or, at least, she
soon will be. People with older children than mine, who
have already had the experience of sharing their parental
responsibilities with the American businessman, do not
seem wholly comfortable about their new partner.

On the other hand, children of my daughter's age are
no longer so intensively conditioned as they once were to
fear and despise the human body. The current practice is
to let them more or less take their own time about toilet

training; nor are they customarily pilloried and condemned for evincing a cheerful interest in their excreta. They see more of their own and other people's living tissue than was formerly the case, and if their innocent inquiries about sex are met with "HUSH! You mustn't *say* that!" it is not because the authorities on child guidance want it that way. I have been rather dazzled, in the course of my maternal duties, at how much protoplasm has come up in the world since I was four years old.

It seems to me quite possible to underestimate the potentiality for good which lies in the freedom of many present-day children from the old-fashioned shame and fear about their bodies. It is freely admitted by all of us that American life is full of tension; but one point about this tension I have never seen raised except in social-science treatises whose vocabulary clearly indicated they were not for the retail trade. That point is that a whole generation of Americans approximately my age had the rug pulled out from under them. These Americans spent their early, formative years—which are now considered very important, but which were just run-of-the-mill then —being indoctrinated with the sinfulness of the flesh and the desirability of chastity. Then, when they reached maturity and what were alleged to be the years of Reason, Freud broke over their unprotected heads. All of a sudden, so to speak, the stakes were changed. All of a sudden, the dictum became—to paraphrase the children's derisive chant—"The last one to be sexually responsive is a bedbug!"

6

This is an exaggerated way of stating that in the first fifty years of the twentieth century, a revolution was taking place in people's thinking. Revolutions are usually untidy and they usually mean that somebody gets hurt. What might be called, very roughly, Freud's Revolution has at length achieved a certain amount of respectability, but it has had a by-product which may need more attention than it gets.

Freud's Revolution has meant that American business and American government are at the present time in the hands of an age group which started life by being made to feel unworthy if it *was* sexual, and arrived at maturity in time to receive a strong, painful and contradictory hint that unworthiness consists of *not* being sexual. This harsh dividing line between the goals of childhood and the goals of adult life is typical of much American living and extends into other areas besides sex and other generations besides mine. It is the key to a good deal of American unhappiness, and American unhappiness is what all compassionate parents want to shield their children from.

In this endeavor, there is one way in which we have a headstart. Childhood has now come to be recognized as a part of living, and is not brushed off, as it once was, as a mere disciplinary prelude to "real life." When one stops to think how slowly, as a general rule, ideas give place to other ideas, this emancipation appears to be a very considerable triumph for the Western European and American mind. In the current emphasis on nuclear fission, it is easy to forget that there are other sciences besides physics; and very possibly we are not sufficiently grateful to the schoolteachers, writers, psychologists, lecturers, thinkers, researchers, anthropologists, philosophers, experimentalists, pediatricians and parents whose combined efforts have given the children lebensraum.

Nobody—at least, nobody important to American middle-class parents—is going to quarrel with the statement that children need love. But this uncontroversial tenet raises a rather troubling question: Where are they going to get it? American children do not live in test tubes and agar solutions. They live in the United States. And in the United States, at the present time, the press, the radio and the popular magazines are hissing and seething and steaming with hostility. Nor is all this hostility directed solely against the Russians. Indeed, as the target for tonight, the Russians very often play second fiddle to such of our countrymen as have not been lucky enough to secure the endorsement of the American communications industry.

It may be that, since I earn my living as a writer, I am oversensitive to changes in vocabulary. It is nevertheless dismaying that the fallible human being—the mortal man who may or may not be right—is disappearing from the American language. People whose opinions and decisions are not popular are more and more referred to in the kind of terms that used to be reserved for cannibals. This fashionable abusiveness passes for patriotism; but the fact is that the disappearance of the fallible human being from the American vocabulary creates unease. It creates unease, moreover, in a far wider area of feeling than the mere region of politics. Some of my best friends are fallible, including me.

However, in matters of political opinion, perhaps a certain amount of hatred is to be expected. What counts, as far as parents and children are concerned, is the extension of this prevalent hostility into the field of entertainment. By their champions, the comics are defended on the ground that they give the child reader a safe, vicarious outlet for his aggression. Nobody, nobody at all, contends that the comics are not all a-bristle with aggression. In a wildly overexcited but by no means wholly dismissable pamphlet, *Love and Death,* a New York printer writing under the pseudonym of G. Legman points up with documentation which cannot be denied the extent to which hostility, violence and aggression have imperceptibly crept into the entertainment with which we adults solace our idle hours.

The traditional man from Mars, if he knew nothing of the American Republic except the so called "mass communications," would certainly be justified in thinking that there is not enough loving-kindness afloat in the contemporary United States to see a crippled old lady across an Indian trail. We live from crisis to crisis, and our sense of dignity is undermined by the recurrent suspicion that at least some of these perils are manufactured—fictional dangers promoted by newspaper publishers, public-relations firms, and men who want to be President.

9

And yet in the midst of this thunderous, denunciatory and singularly unaffectionate atmosphere, the parents and teachers keep up a little cricketlike chirping about children needing love. Are we fools? In spite of the evidence, I do not believe so. But if we are not, then it must be taken as proved that the outward and immediately visible appearance of American life is misleading.

In the old, Pre-World-War I days, respectable, middle-class American parents did what was known as "planning for the children's future." Two factors have intervened, in the years since, to put a considerable crimp in that forward-looking activity. One is that we no longer have the extended periods of peace and prosperity upon which such planning was based. Depressions, inflations and wars succeed each other much more rapidly than they used to. The other factor is that Freud's Revolution has brought it home to the middle class that a child's *present* is his future. It is now generally agreed, by the people we consult about our children, that what a child is going to do about marriage, work, money, friendship and parenthood is to a large extent determined a good many years before he is actually old enough for those performances.

In a nutshell, this means that parents have much more influence on their children than had previously been supposed—twenty or thirty or forty years ago. "Bad blood" or natural "orneriness" is no longer enough to account for the disappointing child. Nowadays everybody turns a gimlet eye upon the cringing mother and father. But to have influence is to suggest that the influence is going to be used in some direction or other. Which direction? This opens up—for parents, at least—an area of great confusion. During the Kefauver Investigation, a Miss Virginia Hill made an extremely favorable impression on television, but the parents of little girls have an understandable reluctance about bending the twig toward that point of the compass. Mr. Whittaker Chambers was embraced by large sections of the press as a hero and a shining patriot, but not many mothers and fathers were disposed to point him out to their children and say, "Go and live a life like that man's." Miss Rita Hayworth, though combining in the highest degree the sterling attributes of beauty and solvency, seems to the alerted parent a forlorn and exploited piece of protoplasm. Senator McCarthy has brought a self-respecting nation almost to its knees, but the average parent hopes rather fervently that no child of his will ever get so spectacularly out of touch with the Marquis of Queensberry.

The conscientious parent of the present day has to be something more than the dutiful saver of pennies for tuition. He has to have more knowledge of both himself and his children than is involved in turning out "well-trained"—to use a word which once had great currency—offspring. Parenthood has become a more complex job than the mere practice of thrift and the inculcation of discipline. What renders the task even more difficult is that it can no longer be done in privacy. It has to be achieved with the whole United States in the living room. Our children are consumers, and it is no more possible to keep producers away from them than it is to divert hummingbirds from honeysuckle.

The United States is my little girl's environment, and it has developed into a much more intense and intrusive environment for children than it was when I was small. As an environmental factor, it deserves at least as much thought and attention as her diet, her schooling, her teeth and her supply of playmates.

It will not be disputed by anybody that what characterizes the American family, as a rule, is the Upward Step. Except for old, rich, long-established families—which are not the concern of this book—we tend, generally speaking, to put horny-handed Grandpa behind us as fast as we can. The familiar pattern in American life is that parents give their children more dentistry, more schooling, more clothes, more recreation, better furniture and a better-balanced diet than they, the parents, themselves had. The Upward Step was a feature of both my husband's family and mine, and we both have reason to be grateful for it. It is nevertheless neither unjust nor unfair to suggest that any given institution has the vices of its virtues.

The Upward Steps of all the American families, taken together, constitute the American standard of living; and for my own part, having once resided for a year in Europe, I am not disposed to abandon that standard of living while I still have strength to put plug in socket. But one serious disadvantage of the Upward Step is that it means parents and children cannot live in the same world. The child starts off on a higher social and economic level than the one his parents inhabited when they were children. Consequently, parents and child do not share a common experience of childhood. To the child, his parents' childhood seems remote, unfamiliar and rather meaningless—if, indeed, he can bring himself to believe that they had one at all. Nor does the gap ever close. If the child grows up into a conscientious, purposeful American who has advanced himself in life, his relationship with his parents in maturity is as necessarily superficial as it was when he was young.

It has been customary, for a long time, to blame this separation of parent and child upon the immigrants. The immigrant child—it has been said—was ashamed of his father, because the old man spoke broken English, and he hastened to put as much distance as possible between himself and his sire. The immigrant child, however, did not disavow his father simply because the progenitor had an imperfect command of the language. He disavowed his father because—since the father was operating in an unfamiliar environment—that father had very little prospect of making lots of money. In those extremely rare instances where the immigrant father, while continuing to speak nothing but fluent Magyar, nevertheless made a million dollars out of a strudel recipe, the children did not feel it necessary to disown him. Poppa became, not a dirty old foreigner, but a charming eccentric.

The immigrants did not impose the Upward Step on the United States. It was the other way around. The United States imposed the Upward Step on the immigrants. The immigrants copied and compounded a kind of behavior they found here upon their arrival. By 1925, the enormous flood of immigration which characterized the nineteenth century had slowed to a mere trickle. The foreign-language press became a dying industry. The Upward Step, however—although it has been a quarter of a century since we had any immigration worthy of the name—is still doing business at the old stand.

The consequence of the Upward Step is that most Americans never form the habit of looking back. They concentrate on the present and the future. And what does this constriction of life into two, instead of three dimensions mean—in terms of human happiness? We have the evidence of two thousand years of literature that the goal toward which human beings have always gravitated—in their quest for contentment and fulfillment—has been knowledge of self. Modern human beings do not go to psychoanalysts because they have symptoms. In a sense, everybody has symptoms. People go to psychoanalysts because they have symptoms they do not understand. It is not the symptoms, but the inability to interpret them, which wears out the springs in those couches.

If knowledge of self is the basis and foundation of happiness, what happens in a forward-thrusting society like ours where the high standard of living involves the loss of the parents? All the books and all the authorities on present-day American parenthood are agreed upon the great influence exerted by parents on children—not only in their actual behavior toward the child, but in their

14

behavior toward each other and in the whole general picture of the kind of people they are. The very large American literature on the subject of child-rearing asserts over and over again that to a certain extent, the children *are* the parents. The children imitate the parents; they identify with the parents; they take over many of the parents' atttitudes and beliefs so thoroughly that they cannot, in later life, completely divest themselves of those attitudes and beliefs—even when they very much want to. The inability of many Southerners to conquer their fear of Negroes, though they may be completely convinced intellectually that it is unnecessary baggage, is a case in point. So is the inability of many women to surrender in sex, although they may be utterly persuaded in their minds that frigidity is an unhealthy symptom.

Even rebellion against the parents is an inverted tribute to their influence. But in our onward-and-upward society, this influence is exercised upon the child by people who start out, and who remain, comparative strangers. Father may possibly, as the early Freudians claimed, bestride his narrow world like a Colossus; but he is also, in our country, The Boy We Left Behind Us. Knowledge of self is indispensable to happiness. Such knowledge does not have to be articulate. It can be unconscious, as it is in a cow or a tiger; but it must be accurate. Knowledge of self, however, is impossible without a fairly exact understanding of the people who had so much to do with forming the self.

In this connection, psychoanalysis has performed a ma-

jor service to Americans of our time in directing attention to the parents. If my own experience of analysis was
a waste of time and money, it was because my particular
practitioners were so enthused about infantile sexuality
and so happily bemused with incest, that they left out of
the picture its most important element. The behavior of
my parents—and, indeed, of most people's parents in the
United States—could be usefully interpreted only in light
of the fact that they were doing what everybody else in
that place and at that time was doing. They were getting
ahead. Psychoanalysts themselves sometimes have a par-
tiality for getting ahead, which may be why some of them
fail to understand that the American family cannot be
treated solely as an arena for Greek tragedy.

My husband and I sometimes speculate on what, in
twenty or thirty years' time, our daughter will think of
us. My own parents saved their money, gave their two
children the college educations they had not had themselves, and achieved an independent old age. They lived
up faithfully to the standards of their time and place,
and those standards, being American, were not the easiest
thing in the world to meet. But their lives, being American lives, did not give them much leisure for meditation,
and I doubt if it ever crossed their minds to wonder what
their children thought of them. In their generation, the
important thing was the parents' opinion of the children,
not vice versa. So far as my husband and I are concerned,
we are not so much interested in our child's thinking
well of us as we are interested in her thinking *something*

about us. And that something, for the sake of her peace of mind, should be as near to the truth as possible.

I cannot hope to convey to my daughter anything of the quality of my own childhood. She is growing up in an American suburb not very far in miles from the respective suburbs where her father and I grew up. But forty years, and the ever-increasing urbanization of American life, have changed the territory beyond recognition. Where her father and I saw open fields, swamps, stretches of woodland and rather amateurish brooks, she sees paved streets, legions of houses, blue spruce and supermarkets. The outward change is no more spectacular than the inner one. Freud's Revolution rendered my childhood—like those of many of my contemporaries—obsolete almost before it was over. I cannot bring up my daughter the way I was brought up. Like most American middle-class parents, I have to bring her up on theories and out of books. I do not regret it, although it seems to me hard on the parents. It represents a step forward in human progress. But it means that my daughter's knowledge of me is a knowledge of my experience in reading books and talking to pediatricians, and not of my experience in being a child.

However, though I cannot convey to my daughter anything of my own outmoded childhood, it has occurred to me more than once in the last four years that I might possibly be able to convey to her something of the quality of her parents' adult life—which is, after all, her present environment. The parents influence the children, but

17

the society influences the parents. My husband and I belong to that large group of Americans who were born in roughly the first twenty or twenty-five years of the current century and whose tribal focus and spiritual pivot was the Great Depression. Twenty or thirty years from now, could my—or anybody's—child go to a library and glean an accurate impression of mid-century America from reading the mid-century "mass communications"? It is my belief that she could not. For one thing, the American press—and its sister institutions—is not wholly free from the vice of self-deception. After the 1948 election, the more intelligent and mentally flexible publicists —like Mr. James Reston, of *The New York Times,* and Mr. Elmo Roper—admitted with commendable frankness that the Delphic oracles and Cumaean sibyls got off the beam because they had been infatuatedly talking to each other, instead of listening to the voters. For another thing, the word "communications" is misleading. "Communication" in the dictionary sense means a two-way exchange. But who ever argues with a movie? Who talks back to *Time* and *Life?* To assume that nobody wants to is taking too much for granted.

If I wish to do a little bit more for my daughter than merely to be the springboard from which she bounces into a penthouse, I shall have to try to give her some glimpse of the pressures that were operating on her mother and father at the time her mother and father were operating on her. This does not mean that anything said about American life in the following pages is to be con-

strued as written by one who has made a conquest of it.
On the contrary. I am not "mature," "adjusted," "well-
integrated," "relaxed" or free from "anxiety"—to employ
the terms which the self-help books have brought into
popular usage. Like most of my fellow countrymen, I
was not raised to be mature; I was raised to be successful.
By the time maturity got on the best-seller list, I was too
old to go back and begin all over again. I was also skeptical enough to wonder about the pure, unalloyed bliss
of being mature in a slightly unripe society. When it
comes to being mature, it does not pay to get too far
ahead of United States Senators, as Mr. Owen Lattimore
found to his cost.

This is therefore not a book which contains any answers.
The most I can aspire to is enough good luck occasionally
to frame the right questions. I have lived all my life in a
transitional society, and I cannot claim to have risen above
that hard conditioning. My mother and father, for example, were the products of a world ignorant of contracep-
tives. In that world, the behavior of men and women toward each other was sternly regulated by the fact that
every act of sexual intercourse might produce a new life
to be taken care of. Sex was not a matter in which there
was much room for experiment. Since my mother and
father brought me up, the pre-contraceptive world is by no
means wholly unfamiliar to me. On the other hand, all the
time I have been old enough to take responsibility, con-
traceptives have been in general use—even, sometimes,
among people whose religion forbids them—and males and

19

females have not had to regard each other as potential dynamite.

The era is well within my memory span when the American middle class believed in work even more than it believed in God. Any kind of work, without reference to its purpose or to what had to be jettisoned in order to get it done.

> "Satan finds some mischief still
> For idle hands to do."

But within the last twenty or twenty-five years, this passionate belief in the absence of idleness has been under attack from two very different quarters. On the one hand, the psychologists have pointed out that work can be compulsive—that it can be just as much of an escape from reality as taking drugs. (It is with me.) On the other hand, the gangsters, publicity men and alumni who buy football players—the "shrewd operators," as they are indulgently called—have caused it to be bruited about that anyone who works is a fool, since money in lavish amounts can be garnered without it. This is quite an egg-dance through which to pick one's way, and I sometimes think rather wistfully of Thoreau's very practical remark on his deathbed— "One world at a time."

If the question is raised—What is the real nature of American life?—can that question be answered wholly without bitterness? Frankly, no. Not by me. In fact, I do not think it ought to be answered completely without bitterness, although bitterness is very much out of fashion at the present time. The only bitterness which is allowed any wide and extensive expression in the United States today is the disillusion consequent upon having joined and left the Communist Party in the thirties. But the failure of the Great Russian Experiment is very far from being the only source of disillusionment in American life.

The failure of many American marriages, the failure of many American sex lives, the failure of many American parents (or children), the failure of many American small businesses, the intermittent failures of American justice— all these produce bitterness, too. That bitterness has to be bottled up. It has no respectable public outlet. Officially, this is the land of opportunity, where happiness lies within reach of anyone who will follow a few simple rules. But bitterness is a part of life. Even American life. The Yankees have not beaten the rap. Bitterness requires to be embraced, lived through and surmounted (if possible)—not ignored.

It is unrealistic not to concede that the Upward Step with which we are all so familiar leaves a certain amount of devastation in its wake. My maternal grandfather was an Englishman who dropped his "h's" and who had the almost spectacular serenity of the British lower classes. I have left him about as far behind as most people have. He worked in a factory and I have a profession. But in the course of this stimulating and typically American ascent, the capacity for contentment seems to have been bred out of me. What I am interested in is whether it can be bred back into my daughter.

Being incurably American, I still think of my daughter

in terms of the Upward Step; but it is an emotional Upward Step rather than a financial one. (Because of our steadily rising price scale, the financial one has become for me—as it has for many Americans—an improbability, anyway.) In this connection, there seem to me to be certain unpublicized and unacknowledged spiritual resources in American life which might be pressed into the service of American children. That I am somewhat lacking in the native compassion which would give my speculations what the blurbs on book jackets call "sweep" and "scope," I am aware. But my guiding star is a not uncheerful line from the Talmud—"It is not upon thee to finish the work; neither art thou free to abstain from it."

II

You Take the High Road and
I'll Take the Middle Class

———

WHEN MY SISTER and I were small children, we did not see very much of my father. He worked in an office all day, came home and ate his supper, and then went out five nights a week to teach mechanical drawing in an evening high school. This exacting regime was almost leisurely, so far as my father was concerned. My paternal grandfather, a contractor, died when my father was fourteen. At that somewhat tender age, my esteemed forebear had to leave school and go to work in a factory. By virtue of unflagging industry and grim determination—and also by virtue of the fact that he was so bright as to engender the suspicion that he had a couple of extra lobes to his brain—my father transformed himself from a factory hand

23

into an architect. This performance was the more remarkable in that, for part of the time, he was the sole support of his mother and his three brothers and sisters. And in those years—this was before the turn of the century—factory hands worked a twelve-hour day.

When I speak of the Upward Step, therefore, I am on home territory. In our family, we are experts at it. But ultimately I reached a point in my own development where I began to realize that mastery of self is a good deal dependent on having accurate memories of the past. Not, as the strict Freudians maintain, just sexual memories—but recollections of the past as a rounded whole and not omitting the massive factor of breadwinning. At this juncture, I found both my parents reluctant to discuss the time when my sister and I were children. Those years had been a period of financial struggle and unremitting hard work, and since they were over, all my folks wanted to do was forget them. They also intimated that, save for the gradual accrual of money in the savings bank, nothing had happened. This was not true, of course. It was not that nothing had happened, but that up and down the streets of our neighborhood, it was not the custom to verbalize about the process of living. Nobody had been trained for it and nobody had much time. Actually, during the closing years of my father's life, I began to suspect that he had done a good deal of thinking in a rather spacious way about the process of life; but by that time, unhappily, his deafness and his ebbing strength did not permit him to communicate very freely.

I have very little reliable information, therefore, about my parents and their times; and most of what I know, I have had to deduce from the imprint left on me. Consequently, I should like to leave some kind of record for my little girl, which she could read in twenty or thirty years time, and which might at least partially illuminate for her the climate in which her personality unfolded. Like a good many other people, I find the present-day United States a rather disturbing and unmanageable place in which to live. In two or three decades, I may be unable or unwilling to remember what times were like when my daughter was a small child. Or, on the other hand, I may be sunk in senile delusions—muttering into my beard that those were the good old days.

When my daughter began to talk, it was frequently suggested to me that I should keep a notebook and write down the cute things she said. On thinking it over, however, it seemed to me that the real pay dirt would be to keep a notebook and write down what the grownups were saying. Since this book is being written, in part, for a reader in the distant future, it may be necessary for me to take issue occasionally with some of the popular prejudices which are now very much in evidence on the surface of American life and which I am convinced are going to look utterly foolish in the strong, cold light of history. Her father and I are not averse to being considered intelligent, at some future time, by the young person we are engaged in rearing. In pursuit of this fair guerdon, it may not be possible to avoid stirring up the all-too-easily-aroused hostility of some of our more emotional citizens.

My second objective in writing this book is to try to work out a sort of philosophy of parenthood which could be used as a basis for the numerous decisions that are such an inescapable part of being a parent. Should we, for instance, buy our little girl things we do not approve of just because all the other children have them? All parents are agreed that they would like to bring up their children to be good human beings; but on the subject of what constitutes a good human being, there is at present a great deal of confusion. The Elizabeth Bentleys and Louis Budenzes have received favorable mention in the press as models of deportment; but since it is not going to be made easy for our children to join the Communist Party, they may find it a little difficult to achieve moral stature by leaving it and then reminiscing punitively about their former associates.

In approaching American life, with a view to pulling together out of it some kind of useful and workable philosophy of parenthood—to say nothing of some not-too-taxing method of getting from the cradle to the grave—two subjects are of primary importance. One of these is money, and the other is the middle class. On the subject of money, I am self-confessedly a little dogmatic. What I know about money, I learned the hard way—by having had it. As to the middle class, I was born and raised in it, and all I ask of World History is that I be given the chance to stay in it. I like middle-class decorum and responsibility, and I do not mind middle-class banality (on those occasions when I am perspicacious enough to recognize it).

However, it must be added that I have not always been this effulgently benign about that station in life to which it pleased God to call me. Twenty years ago, when I was first out of college, all the young folks with git-up-and-git were splashing around with joyous bitterness in the wash from H. L. Mencken. When it was the intellectual fashion to take the hide off the bourgeoisie, I went right along with the crowd. I had at that time, toward the middle class, the unfaltering contempt it is possible to entertain only toward relatives. What happened to change my attitude was a circumstance beyond my control. I learned to appreciate the middle class by being unexpectedly pitchforked out of it.

When I was twenty-eight, I had the experience of seeing my first book suddenly become a popular best seller. The book had not been planned or written with that toothsome fate in mind. In fact, it had never been any part of my plan to be a writer at all. All the time I was in school, my English teachers said that I wrote well. When they occasionally mentioned to my father that I ought to be a writer, he said amiably, "There's no money in it." This does not mean that my father was a dull, insensitive clod. Any householder on our street would have said exactly the same thing—and with equal amiability. On the social level where I grew up, writers were people like Dickens and Thackeray, not people one knew.

This was, of course, before the days of the Book-of-the-Month Club, the Literary Guild and the munificent salaries paid to Hollywood scriveners. This was the Andrew Carnegie Benevolent and Philanthropic Public Library Era. In that era, and in the middle class, there was a sort of vague notion that authors lived in garrets on cheese rinds and bread crusts, in return for which deprivation, they became very famous after they were dead. It is not surprising that, with this background, I did not entertain the notion of being a writer. I have always had an unconquerable prejudice against enjoying things posthumously.

After I got out of school, I went to work and in a few years I married. I married an English teacher who agreed with all the others that I wrote well, and this particular English teacher had a piece of equipment not usually vouchsafed to the members of that profession. He had a brother who was a publisher. Very shortly after we were married, my husband got an exchange professorship in England and we went to live in Devonshire for a year. In Devonshire, I soon found time hanging heavy on my hands. The house we rented was very competently taken care of by a maid, and on my dizzy social eminence as a professor's wife, I could not lay hand to broom without ruining the British caste system. (This was prewar England, of course.) Only two activities were open to me. I could take calves'-foot jelly to the deserving poor, or I could ride to hounds. The poor, however, did not seem overly enthusiastic about the ministrations of even the English ladies, and I had a rather clearly defined impression that they could muddle through without me. As to the horses, their ability to dispense with the Frau Professor was in the nature of a fine art. The horses terrified me.

At this juncture, my brother-in-law suggested that I occupy myself by keeping a diary of my experiences in England, and he gave the discussion a serious note by sending me a small advance. It did not occur to me, when I was writing it, that the book would sell. The casual reflections of a somewhat inexperienced young woman, willing to eat her head off any place but in a stable, did not seem very promising commercially. The most I hoped for was that the volume would do well enough so that the publisher would not be out of pocket for the advance. When I returned to the United States and handed in the manuscript, the publisher said he would not be out of pocket. He said the book was to be called *With Malice Toward Some,* and he said that it would sell. In this opinion, he was alone. No one else shared his optimism. But he was right. He was very, very right; and overnight I was catapulted into the ranks of the Terribly Solvent.

This was the American Dream—the sudden, juicy, delicious, enthralling, entrancing, exhilarating acquisition of money. It cannot be said that I rose magnificently to the occasion. I was confused. The Upward Step I had been used to for three generations; but this was not a step—it was a pole vault. I had not gradually built up a public by writing several books over a long period of years. I acquired a public between Sunday night and Monday morning. They had not had any chance to get to know me, nor

I them, and the glances I cast in their direction were more than a little uneasy. I did not know just exactly what they wanted of me, but whatever it was, I was pretty sure I could not do it. I knew that as far as writing was concerned, I was a talented amateur and not a professional; but this was a guilty secret I could not induce anyone to share with me. The money *proved* I was a professional. Actually, the money proved nothing except that I was a fool for luck—and it was at this point that I began to get the first intimation of a kind of split or division in American life which is to be dwelt on at more length in subsequent chapters.

My vision at this time in my life was the reverse of hawklike, but I could see that it seemed to be taken for granted that what I had inadvertently accomplished was just a beginning—that having polevaulted out of middle-class obscurity and the middle-class income group, I would bend every effort to make the vault stick. The obvious way to do this was to write a couple of sequels to or variations on the original Opus of Opulence, while my name was still "hot," and ultimately to end up in Hollywood or radio as a prosperous fugitive from self-contempt. But I was written out. The vein had not been very large in the first place, and whatever had been in it was gone. If, as I suspected at the time, I was a one-book writer, I wanted to be the kind of one-book writer who writes only one book.

It was not until some years later that I was able to understand where I got this faintly un-American notion. It came from the way I was brought up. It was, in fact, a cultural heritage, since my upbringing was not a system invented by my mother and father especially for me. A great many other Americans my age and older were reared in approximately the same way. I am not nostalgic for my childhood, but my childhood is certainly nostalgic for me. Owing to my early conditioning, I was unable to reap a big, fat harvest of self-confidence from the "fame" attendant upon the first few months of the book's sale. I kept having an uneasy recollection of the woman who lived next door to us saying—apropos of someone whose name was much in the papers—

> "Fools' names and fools' faces
> Always appear in public places."

Nor could I embark with nonchalant grace upon a new and splendid standard of living, on the assumption that I was so full of successful books, I would have no trouble paying for it. Up to the time of the pole vault, I had had too narrow and self-protective a life to have acquired any children or any debts—I have since relaxed my vigilance enough to achieve both—so the money from my first book was, to me, capital. If there was one thing above another that was bred into my bones, it was that respectable people NEVER go into capital—and this applies to emotional, ethical and spiritual capital, as well as financial.

However, I did go into capital—both kinds. I did all the things the fallible human beings usually do, under pressure. I got a divorce, which is standard. I went to a psycho-analyst—which is standard, too. I listened to all kinds of advice. I had to listen to advice, because I was not writing. I was in the uninhabitable position, for an American, of being a demonstrated money-maker who was not making money. Countless schemes were advanced to make it "easy" for me to write. It was suggested frequently that since my first book had been a somewhat rough-and-ready commentary on the English, the next step was to buy a ticket to some other hapless commonwealth and give it the benefit of my bracing and salubrious remarks. But I did not want to.

People with strict Victorian upbringings—and our tribe is still quite a way from having died out—often tend to be very compliant outwardly and very rebellious inwardly. After my first book came out, I tried—in fact, I put myself through all sorts of agonizing contortions—to do what seemed to be expected of me, as far as writing was concerned. A long time afterwards I realized that for all the seeming docility, I had never, underneath, had the slightest intention of going anybody's way but my own.

In retrospect, it is fairly easy to see what, in the years after my first book was published, I was actually doing and what was actually happening to me. While the book was still fresh in people's minds, I was what is known on Broadway as "a property." In this capacity, I encountered somewhat dramatically certain basic American beliefs about money and human beings which, had I remained in modest circumstances, I would have experienced only as a long, dull ache—a chronic perplexity and a permanent sense of disjointedness. It is to these basic American beliefs about money that I am particularly anxious to draw my daughter's attention.

What I was actually doing, in those years which should —theoretically—have been a time of pure felicity, was hanging on blindly to the notion of writing as a talented amateur. Some dim, unformulated instinct warned me that the status of the average professional writer in the United States leaves a little something to be desired. Either he gets paid too much for writing harmless, lukewarm insipidities, or he tries to tell the truth as he sees it and starves to death—which, of course, removes him from the ranks of the professionals. I wanted to keep my independence—my amateur standing, as it were—and to be free to write or not write, when and upon such topics as I myself should choose. Since I did not, at the time, understand this myself, I naturally experienced a little difficulty in communicating it to other people.

I did not depart from the company of the Terribly Solvent with the same meteoric suddenness which characterized my arrival in that sphere, but I departed. There are various ways, and I used most of them. Also, I married again—on this occasion not in such unchastened ignorance of what holy matrimony requires in the way of give and take. By that time, the United States was at war. My husband was in the Army; the air was full of talk about democracy—a distinguishing characteristic of American society being that it is the most verbal in the world; and I went to work in a very minor administrative capacity at the widely celebrated Stage Door Canteen.

It is possible that there is some one basic factor in American life which would explain why American tension affects the whole population and not just parts of it. There is a hint of such a factor in the circumstance that any given American has to switch back and forth a thousand times a day from the fact of his life, as his five senses know it, to the fiction of his life as it is uninterruptedly portrayed by the press, radio, movies, television and popular magazines. Very few American men know—much less marry— women who look like movie stars. No American of either sex, however, gets much chance to forget what a movie star looks like. The kitchens and bathrooms we see in the magazines and the cinema are stainless, radiant and without flaw. The ones we actually occupy contain the usual sediment of living.

We know of our own knowledge that we are human beings, and, as such, imperfect. But we are bathed by the communications industry in a ceaseless tide of inhuman, impossible perfection. Upon ordinary human beings, this inescapable bath of perfection has one of two effects. Either they feel permanently dejected and unworthy because they have failed to live up to what (they assume) everybody else has been able to live up to, or else they knock themselves out trying to earn sufficient money to command such perfection. In either case, their capacity for enjoyment is irretrievably crippled.

The Stage Door Canteen was a good example of the unnerving discrepancy between the fact and the fiction of American life. Through the mistaken generosity of the communications industry, it was publicized throughout the length and breadth of the land as a place where the celebrities of stage, screen and radio—the Flowers of the Forest—donned percale aprons and made sandwiches for the servicemen with their own hallowed digits. The Flowers of the Forest, however—at least, those of them who would have significance for a Pfc. from Selma, Alabama—do not lead the kind of lives which permit them to put in long hours of humble toil. They move around a lot, and they have contractual obligations.

Actually, the Stage Door Canteen made a very meaningful contribution to American life. It was one of the very few canteens in the country—I know of only two others—where Negro servicemen were entertained on the same terms as white servicemen. The purpose of the Canteen was recreational. So far as Allied victory was concerned, this purpose was something less than the keystone of the arch. The Canteen, however, gave a certain resolute and full-bodied air to itself by entertaining all the servicemen and not just the white ones. To pull off this democratic coup in a prevalently discriminatory Republic was a triumph of no mean proportions. But the public prints, with a few honorable exceptions, ignored it.

I do not mean to suggest that the Flowers of the Forest lay down on the job. They did not. They came when they could, and they very sensibly stuck to their last, which was to be diverting, and eschewed the fabrication of sandwiches. But the AUS was something more than a pint-sized Army, and there were not enough Flowers to go around. My point is not concerned with anybody's individual behavior, but with the fact that the Canteen illustrated, in miniature, the necessity Americans are under to live in two worlds at once. The fiction about the Stage Door Canteen was, at that time, familiar to everyone. The fact—that it was only mildly glamorous, but it was boldly democratic—almost never got into the papers. The people who went there, however—both civilian and military—could scarcely help being aware of the reality, no matter what they might have just finished reading in a magazine or newspaper. The permanent conflict between fact and fiction of which this is an infinitesimal sample means that the people who are caught in the middle—150,000,000 of them—have to live out their lives on permanently unsure ground.

If the Flowers of the Forest did not draw the tea, empty the ashtrays and dance with the lonely servicemen, who did? These indispensable services were performed, nobody will be surprised to learn, by people from the middle class. The entertainment industry, which founded and ran the Canteen, is as well stocked with middle-class people as the Air Force is with ground crews. The vigilant reader has no doubt already noticed that I have made no effort to define what I mean by the middle class, and beyond describing it as a rough grouping which excludes both race-track touts and cartelists, I do not intend to. Anyone who uses the phrase at all, knows what he means by it and does not want to be told by me. I think, however, I shall not be strewing around any Apples of Discord if I say that the

people in the middle class are the people whose formative
years were not spent in the corrosive shadow of far too
much or far too little money. I have rather lightly waived
definitions and delimitations because essentially, being in
the middle class is a feeling as well as an income level.

During the four years of its existence, three million servicemen passed through the Stage Door Canteen, so the
people who worked there had the opportunity to become
acquainted with quite a sizeable handful of their fellow
countrymen. In addition, it was more or less inevitable to
develop a large correspondence with the servicemen. Since
the Canteen was for enlisted men, and was not open to
officers, the clientele was not generally the product of what
the class magazines call Gracious Living. We got more
comic-strip readers than lean-minded strategists. For me,
as for many other people there, the Canteen was a develop-
mental experience. I saw more Americans—Caucasian and
otherwise—than I had ever seen in my life. It did what all
the plans, schemes and conferences—as well as the expensive psychoanalysis—had failed to do. It took me back to
writing.

In those days, as I have said, the air was full of talk
about democracy. At the Canteen, and so far as the servicemen were concerned, the air was also full of anti-Semitism.
About the crudely anti-Jewish remarks tendered me by
servicemen, I could not very well take a holier-than-thou
attitude. I was myself brought up to be anti-Semitic. In my
childhood, Jews were usually referred to as kikes; the remark, "That's the Jew of it for you," was current and

37

prevalent; and it was taken for granted that the Jewish confraternity consisted of a threatening multiplicity of Fagins whose aim in life was to humiliate and destroy the seraphic congregation of the Gentiles. This is what I was taught, and there was no one around who questioned or contradicted. My instructors were not evil people. They were simply passing on what they themselves had never heard questioned. The anthropologists call it cultural conditioning.

It was not until I grew up and moved out into a more complex environment that I met any Jews, and they were so unlike Fagin that I refused to believe they were Jewish. When I could finally be convinced on the point, it was my wont to tell them with sweet condescension that, of course, they were not like the other Jews. Some years later, the pukka sahibs made me buy that one back by telling me with sweet condescension that, of course, I was not like the other Americans. Two factors changed me from being anti- to what I might almost call pro-Semitic. One was actually meeting Jews and having the evidence of my eyes and ears that they were not like Fagin. The other was meeting Gentiles whose opinion I valued and who disapproved of anti-Semitism. My early training in anti-Semitism had been external and more or less automatic, and since I came from the sheltered and non-embittered middle class, I had no pressing emotional reason for clinging to it.

If many of the servicemen were anti-Semitic, I understood perfectly well what had made them that way. I could not, however, be happy about it or dismiss it from my mind. In the ordinary way, one can simply stay away from people whose views produce discomfort. But I was working in a canteen, and I was pinned to the spot. No profounder morality or ethics exist in my character than can be picked up through a routine processing by the Episcopal Church and the public schools of Yonkers, New York, but I felt a deep personal involvement in the meaning of the war. In those days—as we all wistfully remember —we had the type of armed conflict about which it was possible to have a wholehearted, unhesitant, one-piece feeling. Under the influence of such a feeling, I blew the dust off my typewriter and wrote, around the theme of anti-Semitism, a novel called *Some Of My Best Friends Are Soldiers* which I hoped was persuasive rather than angrily didactic. It was quite different in content and attitude from my first book, but there was quite a difference between the peacetime and the wartime world.

Until I worked at the Stage Door Canteen, I was not aware that the position occupied by ethics and morality in the United States is a somewhat odd one. It was to be expected that some parts of the population would be openly hostile to the Canteen's racial equality. What was surprising—at least, to me—was the number of people who were patronizing about it. Theoretically approving, they nevertheless referred to it with tolerant amusement as a "good cause." Up until that time, I had not noticed that when an American uses the phrase "good cause," he invariably condescends to it. The condescension is not studied or deliberate. It is simply that that is the way everybody inflects those words. But what lies behind the condescension? What explains it?

If good causes are mildly amusing with the faintest dash of contemptibleness, are bad causes admirable? Patently, no. Or, is the feeling that there should be no causes at all? This probably comes closer to it. And yet here we all are, living day in and day out, from one end of life to the other, in a country whose social structure is mainly a series of "good causes" elevated into political institutions. One would think that such a hidden contradiction might cause trouble. It does. Here is another intimation of a rift or split in American life—another hint of a universal difficulty which would explain why American tension afflicts all classes and groups so uniformly.

Apropos of contradictions, it would seem logical that since I was brought up to be anti-Jewish, I would also have been reared to take the traditionally unflattering view of Negroes. But in the sparsely settled suburb where I grew up, Negroes were so incredibly remote that it was not necessary to have any opinions or feelings about them at all. In our neighborhood, nobody had servants. A woman, generally Polish, who came in once a week to do the laundry or the heavy cleaning was the extent of our experience with caste and class. Until I got to college and took sociology courses, nobody tried to influence me in any direction at all about non-Caucasians. I was pretty much of a clean slate. The professors made a theoretical equalitarian of me, but when I went to the Canteen, I was like most white Americans in that I had never met any Negroes socially.

If it had been as easy as it sounds to run an unsegregated canteen, there would have been more of them. The pressures of the time were on the side of segregation. To resist these pressures, and to keep on resisting them, required unflagging work by a considerable group of Negroes and whites. It seemed to me unfair that the Flowers of the Forest should get so much credit for being patriotic, while these devoted people were overlooked. There was the further circumstance that in several years of dealing with all shades and brands of anti-Negro feeling, these people had acquired a body of valuable experience. Since there were plenty of other situations where this experience could be used, it seemed too bad for it to vanish into thin air when the war was over. For these reasons, I wrote a third book, *Color Blind,* which was about the Stage Door Canteen's little-known but extremely helpful contribution to the practical ethics of the Western Republic.

Six years elapsed between the publication of my first and second books, and in those six years the United States changed from a nation at peace to a nation at war. In time of war, a nation re-examines its morality. It has to. People do not fight because they have know-how. They fight because they have convictions. The change from peace to war, with its consequent re-emphasis on ethics, explains how I could start out as a carefree humorist and end up writing about anti-Semitism and racial equality.

It is only recently that my wish not to belong to the

strenuous circles of the Terribly Solvent has become conscious and articulate. Unconsciously, however, I must have entertained it for a long time. For, if an American writer wants to stay in the middle class, anti-Semitism and racial equality are two subjects that will do it for him. At least, they would some years ago. This was before the time of *Gentleman's Agreement* and the Hollywood movies on race. On the other hand, and fortunately for me, the American spirit is sufficiently troubled and the American ethos sufficiently ingrained, so that I have not up to now had to drop out of the middle class via the trap door at the bottom.

If I were reading this book instead of writing it, politeness might constrain me from asking out loud what exactly happened to the money from that first book; but the question would certainly pass through my mind. The final bit of the glittering pile got used up last year, when my husband and I bought—or, at least, started to buy—a six-room house in the suburbs so that our little girl could have fresh air and a good public-school system. I lived on my emoluments for some years. I did not live lavishly, as lavishness is understood in the environs of Madison Avenue and 57th Street, but I did not put myself to the trouble of saving wrapping paper and the string from packages. I took expensive vacations. There is nothing to make a vacation costly like the fact of having very little, except the Inner Woman, to take a vacation from.

A considerable amount of the money I gave away—a procedure which resulted, in almost every instance, in a measure of bitterness between me and the donees. I have always been rather slow and laborious about sizing up my fellow men, and when I was younger, I was willfully prone to see in people what I wanted to see, and not what was actually there. What went wrong between me and the recipients of my bounty was the circumstance that in a money society, there is one thing you cannot successfully do with money. You cannot give it away. It is too important. My beneficiaries, though convinced that they were delighted with the windfall, were unconsciously ill at ease with themselves for having taken it. As for me, my own unconscious attitude was that I had bought the creatures and they were mine. If anyone had pointed this out to me at the time, I would have denied it hotly. No one did point it out to me, however, because I had money; and when you have money, people are inclined to be a little careful what they say to you. Unpalatable truths take longer to catch up to the well-heeled than to the indigent.

Another large segment of the money I sank into psychoanalysis. It was analysis of the now somewhat obsolete type which a witty friend of mine refers to as Oedipus-Bedipus. At the time, I considered this a very wise and shrewd investment—an opinion in which the analysts heartily concurred—but on looking back at it, I am inclined to think that this was the only part of the money which was really wasted. With the rest of it, I may be said to have purchased experience; and as everybody knows, that comes high.

However, all that is now, in every sense of the word, water over the dam. Currently, I am engaged in thinking,

43

as parents do, about my daughter. In this connection, both money and the middle class must be regarded as subjects of major importance. Money, and its place in the American scheme of things, deserves extended treatment. As to the middle class, when I say that all I want is to be able to stay in it, the wish is accompanied by a considerable apprehension that it may not be granted. As our inflations succeed each other with ever-increasing rapidity, it costs more and more money to stay in the middle class. It is also beginning to take more and more courage to come out in support of middle-class standards of virtue.

We in the United States are now going through the painful process of seeing virtue redefined. Ex-Communists, confessing their own and other people's sins in a blaze of publicity, have taken the place once occupied (with considerably more reticence and self-sufficiency) by Nathan Hale. The middle-class virtues of responsibility, honesty and decorum are passing out of the hands of the middle class. They are not passing into the hands of any other class. They are just passing. Period. Why? Perhaps an exploration of the basic nature of American life, as opposed to the immediately visible surface, will provide an explanation.

III

The Five O'Clock Shadow
over the United States

———

Viewed freshly, and as if one had never till this moment seen it before, the most visible thing about the United States is that it is a business and "success" society. The point deserves special emphasis. Our Republic is not a pastoral, not a military, not an agricultural, not a nomadic, not a clerical, but a business civilization. Nor is there anything random, casual or accidental about the United States as a business society. It is thoroughly well integrated—organized from top to bottom for the maximum efficiency of commerce and industry, for the maximum efficiency of making money. We are so accustomed to the infiltration of business into every single area of human living that we take it for granted. It seems to us the natural, the inevitable—indeed, the only conceivable—way for a nation to be organized. How far this is from the truth, however, is evident the moment we stop to reflect that most of the rest of the world does not live the way we do.

There are, of course, other business societies—England, Holland, Belgium and France, for instance. But ours is the only culture now extant in which business so completely dominates the national scene that sports, crime, sex, death, philanthropy and Easter Sunday are money-making propositions. This statement is not to be interpreted as critical or derogatory. In this book, there are no villains, although the heroes may not be just exactly the people we have been asked to regard as heroic. Mechanistically considered, the American business society has been a brilliant and unparalleled success. No view of that society can be valid which does not acknowledge that its distinctive quality— its unique triumph and the thing which sets it apart from other societies—is the actual and potential freedom from drudgery which it has bestowed on the human race. Not that the United States invented the business society. We borrowed it from Western Europe. But with the passion and energy which have always characterized American activity, we developed it to lengths which left the originators gasping.

I am more intense than casual about this semi-divine gift of freedom from drudgery because I am one of its direct beneficiaries. I do my own housework. From 9:00 A.M. to 2:00 P.M. a woman—for whose calm and stable and generous character I can never be sufficiently grateful—comes in to take care of my little girl while I address myself with what scraps of diligence I can muster to my typewriter. This woman does the breakfast dishes, makes the beds and tidies up, but her principal job is to take care of my daughter. The shopping, cooking, heavy cleaning, gardening, mending, moth-proofing and curtain-making, I do myself. (Or leave undone, and fret about.) In these activities, I can count on some slight assistance from my husband. My husband, however, is in the academic world; and although he is not a full professor, he has a full professor's absent-mindedness. His grasp of abstract concepts is superb, but rakes and mops are likely to drop with a clatter from his limp and meditative fingers.

Drudgery—or rather, the absence of same—is part of my daily living. Moreover, I am old enough to remember when people cleaned rugs by throwing them over a clothesline and beating them with a stick. Cooking on a coal range, boiling clothes in big tubs, making Javelle water to bleach them, heating flatirons, and washing down woodwork with soap which then had to be rinsed off were, when I was growing up, the usual procedures. A day does not pass, therefore, that I do not feel profoundly grateful to the American business society for its production and distribution of the vacuum cleaner, the steam iron, the pressure cooker, the automatic laundry, the home permanent, the electric sewing machine and the luxurious detergent. It is indisputable that the geographical and cultural entity which we call the United States has smoothed the way and lightened the burdens of millions of its own people, and has made physically possible, at least, the amelioration of toil for all the rest of the planet.

But James Watt did not invent the steam engine in order to make a fast buck. And in the United States, the Industrial Revolution began as a creative and continent-conquering impulse. However, it became very evident, very quickly, that there was money to be made from these inventions. A great deal of money. And so business took over. Big Business. The unparalleled dominance of business in American life is not in the least bit affected by the fact that nonindustrial pockets are to be found here and there in the American scene. On his summer vacation, the American sometimes goes to a little fishing village or a farm community or a North Woods settlement, and he suffers a considerable wistfulness as he observes the placid inefficiency—by industrial standards—which characterizes these backwaters. The entertainment industry occasionally selects for the full treatment one of these nonindustrial pockets, on the assumption that the life which is lived there represents the American Way. But the American Way is the business way—the high-pressure, producing-and-consuming, making-a-profit way—and the quiet backwaters provide nothing in significant quantities except grass roots, grass and nostalgia. They have no influence at all on the prevailing moral and psychological climate of the United States, which is the climate of a business society.

So much emphasis is placed, by the American press and radio, on "free" or "private" enterprise and the "independent" businessman, that it is hard for Americans to think of themselves as living in a society at all. The official picture of us is the picture of a collection of invulnerable hermits, piling up money in a state of contented anarchy. However, the picture is not true. Compared to the business societies of Western Europe, ours is a somewhat lawless one. Gangsterism, the Ku Klux Klan, the Vigilantes, the institution of lynching and our universal evasion of the Prohibition Amendment are evidence that our business society has a strain of recklessness not apparent in, for instance, the English business society. In its April, 1948, issue, *Fortune* ran an article comparing English and American banking and pointing rather pridefully to the fact that American banking is more reckless than its British counterpart. But the American business society actually is a society—even though we do not usually think of it that way—and as such, it does the two things that all societies, of any description, do.

For one thing, it moves. It changes. There is no such thing as a society that does not move. Sometimes, like those of the Pueblo Indians, societies move with glacial slowness; but they always move. Yet at this point in American history, both the responsible and the irresponsible press are in accord on one point. They are agreed that from the economic, political and moral standpoint, the United States is a nation in aspic—changelessly, movelessly and immutably good. Or with only such minor and disarming faults as nobody need bother with. Only in the field of mechanical progress—only in the matter of flying

49

from New York to London overnight, or buying I.B.M. machines for the universities to mark the True-or-False tests—is it conceded that there is any movement, or any need for movement, in the American scene. However, the American business society moved from a nineteenth-century laissez-faire economy to the New Deal and the concept of the welfare state. This transmutation took place in spite of passionate insistence by most of the news-gathering industry that it could not and would not happen.

Save for feeling comfortably superior to the people who had to get around in surreys with a fringe on the top, Americans are not encouraged to look backward and digest the past. It nevertheless requires no great, wrenching effort of the intellect to accept the fact that the American business society, like all societies, moves. Also like all societies, it never leaves the people in it alone. Any society —advanced or "primitive"—perpetually influences and puts pressure on its individual members to be something or do something they would not have thought of by themselves. A society has to do this, if it is going to keep itself going as a distinct and recognizable community. Consequently, all societies, with no exceptions, impose a certain degree of standardization upon their component human beings. Some impose more than others, but a certain minimum of regimentation—traffic lights, for instance, for a people that moves on wheels—is necessary, or the civilization could not exist at all.

It is not surprising to find, therefore, that a clerical society puts pressure on its individuals to be religious persons; a traditionally agricultural society influences its individuals to be good farmers; and a business society endeavors to mold its individuals into the pattern of the successful businessman. Thus, a clerical society fosters prevalent attitudes among its people of humility and passivity; an agricultural society turns out more people who are patient and stable than people who are not; and the "typical" man in a business-success society is aggressive, competitive and skeptical. The climate, the general atmosphere, of a business society, therefore, is predominantly aggressive, competitive and skeptical.

To be sure, since the American business society has what might be called a tie-in sale with Christianity, the psychological attitudes it encourages are not so bluntly labeled. They are described as "being on the ball," "going places," "getting ahead," "being a live wire," or being "hardheaded." Sometimes, in fact, American business encourages people to be aggressive, not by celebrating aggression as such, but by heaping scorn on the nonaggressive and noncompetitive. Such persons are spoken of as "never having met a payroll," "muddleheaded," "starry-eyed," and "unrealistic."

The sensitive American may perhaps wince a little at hearing his country described as prevailingly aggressive, competitive and skeptical, but it should be kept in mind that these qualities are not necessarily bad. They are good or bad according to the situation in which they are used. In one context, American aggression, competitiveness and skepticism have produced for the United States a body of technical achievement unrivaled in human history, and that achievement has made life cleaner, safer and more comfortable for millions of people who would have had harder—and shorter—lives before the American industrial machine got rolling. Furthermore, no single person or group of persons, however influential, creates a social climate. Social climates are created unconsciously and unwittingly. Our social climate is created by books, movies, plays, newspapers, gossip, hearsay, radio, ritual, comics, tradition, television, magazines, lecturers, old wives' tales, schools, churches, house organs, parental training, advertising, habit, custom, convention and conversation.

Nobody, literally nobody, rises above the society he lives in. The people who seem to have the most to do with molding American opinion—the so-called policy-makers—are just as much victims as victimizers. In fact, they are likely to be much more the inadvertent captives of the society and its climate than some of the humbler folk whose thinking they aspire to direct. Aggression, competitiveness and skepticism are—in the United States—what the social scientists call prevailing cultural attitudes. Nobody can take much credit for a cultural attitude when it is good, and nobody can be blamed for it when it is bad. Cultural attitudes are almost literally in the very air we breathe. They are as catching as the measles, and they imply no more personal responsibility than is suggested by succumbing to a germ or getting sunburned in the sunlight.

Since American business has always been considered

more or less sacred—by Americans, at any rate—and since at the present time it is regarded as especially blasphemous and "Communistic" to hint at any flaw in it, perhaps I had better assure those of my readers who are getting nervous that I was raised by a Roosevelt-hating Republican and I was myself trained for a business career. My father, though aggressive as a buzz saw and skeptical as Pontius Pilate, was not in business. But he had a profound admiration for the business society's efficiency and, himself endowed with a good head for figures, its arithmetic seemed to him downright seductive. For his first-born, the undersigned, he had even more—and more personal—affection. In consequence, nothing could be more natural than that a business training seemed to him the one sure and certain guarantee of my prolonged security, safety and general welfare.

It was not my own choice. My father handed down to me a considerable measure of his own aggressiveness, but neglected to pass on his mathematical gift. As a young person, I was considerably confused on the subject of what I wanted to be or to do, but the nearest thing I had to a clear idea on the subject was a notion that I would like to teach English. It was the English that attracted me, rather than the teaching—but I did not know that at the time. The idea that I might merely get married and continue the human race was not, in our household, given much attention. My father was all his life wistful about people who had had a chance to get more education than he had, and I was under a good deal of pressure to get high marks in school. When I got them, I became too promising a sprig to be heaved without a second thought into the cistern of domesticity. Marriage was not ruled out, but it was clearly secondary.

On the subject of my career, therefore, I was not extensively consulted. This does not mean that my father wanted to ride roughshod over me, or that he did not have a considerable capacity for being fond of people. He died of arterio-sclerosis—an infirmity in which, toward the end, the mind wanders. I went into his room one afternoon, four days before he died, and said, "Hi, Pop, it's Margaret. Do you know me?"

He shot me a bright glance.

"No," he said, "but I'd like to buy you a beer."

Twenty-five years ago, the idea that "Father knows best" had more currency and more prestige than it does now. Also, my father's grueling early years had left him with a permanent habit of anxiety—some of it wore off, in the later years of his life—and one of the things he was anxious about was his children. My approach to business, therefore, is not the approach of one who ever twinkled in the bright firmament of liberal arts. When I went to college, I took a course called Secretarial Science, and my curriculum was principally concerned with typing, shorthand, office practice, personnel management, statistics, double-entry bookkeeping, business law and similar down-to-earth subjects.

If it has been established, as I hope it has, that this writer is not a "sensitive" artist condescending to business, we may now safely return to the topic of the American business society and the fact that it is undeniably flying distress signals. The tension in American life is a puzzling phenomenon. There seem to be so few visible reasons for it. It is too easy, and it accomplishes nothing, to explain it as based solely on fear that the Russians will drop atom bombs on us. We have the evidence of all our major novelists—Dreiser, Hemingway, Faulkner, Fitzgerald, Sinclair Lewis and Mark Twain—that American tension was a recognized infirmity long before the atom bomb was invented.

From the point of view of its practicing fathers and mothers, our country seems less a nation in aspic than a nation in trouble. Within the past decade, 350,000 schoolteachers have been forced out of the profession by the meagerness of their salaries and in some cases by overbearing interference in their personal lives. To the non-white American, it is cold comfort that the Congresses which failed to pass any civil rights legislation were elected by the secret ballot in a two-party system. (In fact, that makes it worse.)

In the United States, three out of every five marriages end in divorce.* One out of every ten Americans spends part of his life in a mental home. We have the highest crime rate in the civilized world. Every year, 35,000 Amer-

---

* To be sure, this figure is a little swollen by the fact that just as we have six-goal polo players, we have three-divorce movie stars and crooners. But it is significant that some of our most conspicuously successful people—who would seem to have the most reason for being placidly satisfied with themselves and their lives—are dogged in their matrimonial careers by what the poet refers to as divine discontent.

icans are killed—this does not include the injured—in automobile accidents. Juvenile delinquency is with us, as it is not with the other business societies, high on the list of admittedly unsolved problems. The American statistics, in short, which have to do with people's personal lives—as distinguished from the cheerful digits on freight-car loadings—show a disturbing pattern of failure, collapse and breakdown.

Obviously, something is out of kilter. Possibly the typically American characteristics of aggression, competitiveness and skepticism are operating in some area where they are not the ideal equipment. And this is just the case. The sanctioned hostility of the American business society achieved its fullest formulation and acceptance in the days of the robber barons, who said, and got away with it, "The public be damned." But the days of the robber barons are over. This is the era of the smooth operator, the public-relations firm, and the sales-sensitive litany that the customer is always right. (This dictum, coldly considered, is certainly the most "unrealistic" statement the Western Hemisphere has yet produced.) With the advent of mass communications, it became just as impossible for the businessman to be aggressive, competitive and skeptical within the privacy of his business as for parents to bring up their children without intrusion in the privacy of the home.

The result is that the "typical" man in our business society, the successful businessman, has an almost impossible role. He must produce the results of hostility without showing any hostility. In a system loosely described as freely competitive, he must produce results—i.e., financial success—which can only be achieved by unco-operative, self-absorbed devotion to his own advancement; but he must produce these results without at any time appearing to be selfish. The Smiler with the Knife, in short. What happens to the apostle of the business society who has a deficient supply of hostility was poignantly set forth in Arthur Miller's play, *Death of a Salesman*.

The American businessman has been much laughed at and, less frequently, has been regarded with pity and compassion—as in *Babbitt*. But to get to the roots of American tension, it is necessary to view him as being just as much the result of social molding and social pressures as the Aleutian Indian. The Aleut is nudged and jostled by his society into being as competent a hunter and fisherman as the state of his reflexes will permit. But all he has to do to the seals and walruses and polar bears is to kill them. He does not also have to make them like him. By disillusioned young novelists and anguished fugitives from the communications industry, American business is often alluded to as a jungle. The fact is that if it really were a jungle, it might be easier to live in. Pythons are not world-weary, and tigers are not cynical.

When privacy disappears from a society, as it is disappearing from ours, it disappears for everybody—for robber barons, divorcées, parents, and up-to-the-minute businessmen, as well as for professors suspected of having Communist sympathies. The businessman in the business society would seem to be the ideal example of the person well suited to his job—the round peg in the round hole, in fact. But even during the business day, the American business-man is compelled to operate under a psychological handicap; and when the business day is over, and he goes home to "relax" with wife, children and friends, his troubles multiply. When the business day is over, the socially trained and socially produced businessman must perforce try to turn off his aggression, competitiveness and skepticism as he would turn off water in a faucet. And, of course, it cannot be done. The weight and pressure of a whole society—and a very well-organized one, at that—cannot be eluded merely by putting on a hat and walking away.

It is perhaps time now to make an explanation which I ought possibly to have made a little earlier. In this book, I am consistently using the word "society" where a social scientist—an anthropologist, a sociologist or a psychologist —would use the word "culture." The professionals make a distinction between a society and a culture—the society being merely the sum total of the human beings in any given group and the culture being the things those human beings think and say and do. Since I am talking about what American human beings think and say and do in their business-dominated country, I should properly refer to the American business culture instead of the American business society.

However, when I was growing up, the word "culture" meant having a sepia photograph of the Coliseum by moonlight hanging over the umbrella stand in the front hall; and I have never been able to teach myself to think of the word in any other way. In the belief that many of my readers may suffer from the same disability, I have chosen to say "society" instead of "culture," although it is technically incorrect. Since it is impossible to be at once scientific and cosy, I have elected to be cosy.

I trust I will be forgiven by the social sciences for this gaucherie—the more particularly since I am very much in their debt. When orthodox psychoanalysis failed to help my insomnia and anxiety, I turned to the public library. In the works—among others—of Abram Kardiner, Margaret Mead, Ruth Benedict, Lewis Mumford, Ralph Linton, Clyde Kluckhohn, Karen Horney, Karl Menninger, Harry Stack Sullivan, Erich Fromm, Wilhelm Reich, Ashley Montagu and David Riesman, I was able to pick up a good many helpful hints and illuminating insights about the forces which gave my life its own particular direction and which may be expected to have their bearing on my little girl.

It is not that all these writers are in sweet, harmonious agreement with each other. They are not. But their writing is a part of that great body of discoveries about what is carelessly called "human nature" which has derived from the pioneering of Sigmund Freud. This body of discoveries has been overshadowed by nuclear fission, but it is nevertheless the proudest and most significant achievement of the last seventy-five or eighty years. It is also the hope—the only hope—for the future. It is a well-known fiction of American life that this is the atomic age. It is a little-known fact of American life that we have in our libraries the definite knowledge of how to turn out good human beings. A little of this knowledge has seeped into the books on child care. A little, but not enough.

That there is nothing in this book which has not already been said in other books, by other writers, will already have become apparent. Scientists, however, are under the necessity—if they are to be clear and true and exact in their results—of developing and using scientific language. The dabbler, the amateur, on the other hand, can afford to be a little more informal; and having myself come many a cropper on things like "acculturation" and "parataxic distortion," I am not inclined to leave them about for other people to stub their toes on.

Very little knowledge of people in other countries is required for seeing that the American family is distinctive in two ways. First, it has more comforts and conveniences than families in other lands, and second, it is more brittle and more fragile—more likely to break under pressure. On the surface, it would appear that modern American inventions have taken family life out of the home and transferred it to more public places. But that is only on the surface.

No civilization yet devised has been able to dispense with the institution of the family. The family can, and does, take on many forms. It was one thing in Sparta—in fact, it was not much in Sparta, and Sparta did not stay the course—and quite another thing in Mandarin China. But in essence, what the family stands for is some kind of clearly defined, well understood, workable relationship between the older people in a society and the younger ones who will eventually take their places. If the race is to continue, if the young of the species are to be raised to maturity, the family in some form or other must exist. It cannot be by-passed.

But the psychological attitudes which are indispensable in the American market place are disastrous to family life. Family life, to be comforting to its participants, has to be based on love, trust and faith. It requires yieldingness, generosity, sympathy, altruism, tenderness—all the qualities, in fact, which lead straight to bankruptcy. Here is the basis of American tension. Here is the reason why bringing up children in the United States, if the parents are conscientious and responsible, is a task pervaded with anxiety and strained uncertainty. American tension is not caused by labor unions, taxes, government spending, Communists in the State Department, nuclear fission, machine technology or turbulence in Asia. It is caused by the fact that the American family is tragically out of gear with the profit structure which has mushroomed up around it. That is why the tension is so general in all classes of society and in people of the most widely divergent views and interests.

Most Americans, without being aware that they have made a choice, follow the directions indicated by the business society and lead family lives of strain, perplexity and unspoken disappointment. (It is, of course, not necessary to be in business to be shaped and influenced by the business society. Merely being alive in it will do the trick.

61

Doctors are frequently businessmen. So are lawyers. So are designers.) Usually, we are not explicitly conscious of the tension in our family lives, but our behavior reveals it. We do not stay home. We stream out in our millions to ball games or movies—where people do not have to talk to each other, and sharing is limited to a bag of popcorn. Or, if we do remain under our own rooftrees, we avoid close family contacts by turning on the radio or television. And we worry about our children.

The heart and core of American chronic unhappiness is the fact that the American family is failing in its job of turning out stable human beings. It is not failing because it has too many machines. It is failing because Americans do not dare to cultivate in themselves those characteristics which would make family life creative and rewarding. To do so, would ruin them financially.

As has already been noted, the business society very often instills profit-making qualities in its members, not by applauding aggression, etc., but by heaping scorn and ridicule on the nonaggressive and noncompetitive. People whose jobs are indispensable, but unlikely to prove stepping-stones to fame and fortune—preachers, teachers, nurses, subway motormen, telephone operators, school janitors, truck drivers, railway switchmen, postmen, milkmen—are spoken of as "public servants," with the emphasis on the "servant." The note of irritated condescension is particularly apparent when members of these callings go on strike. A very good job can be done of bolstering up private enterprise merely by the reiterated assertion that public enterprise is the province of fools and weaklings.

However, the crucial disadvantage of aggression, competitiveness and skepticism as national characteristics is that these qualities cannot be turned off at five o'clock. They can be repressed, of course, after the business day is over. In fact, they usually are. But this means that the people who do the repressing are restless, haunted and uncomfortable without knowing why. They smoke too much, eat too much, drink too much, buy too much, marry too much, take too many sleeping pills and drive too fast. Stark tragedy would be easier to bear. Time ultimately dims the pain of bereavement, but a permanent, undiagnosed tension yields to nothing but death.

As every schoolboy knows, repressed emotions do not evaporate. They merely find their way to the surface in devious and twisted forms. The single most important problem of the American business society can be quite simply stated—though not quite so simply resolved. That problem is the aggression, competitiveness and skepticism which have no place to go after five o'clock, and which spill out in all directions—not only conventionally against Russia and the Communists, but also against liberals, Negroes, government employees, schoolteachers, artists and children. It is a point worthy of special note that this surplus hostility—this unemployed aggression—is directed not only against people who are openly hostile to the business society, like the Communists, but also against people who are merely indifferent to it.

It may seem surprising to mention children as one of

the groups toward whom the surplus hostility of the business society is directed. This does not mean that the individual American is hostile to any individual child. On the contrary, he may be markedly generous in his personal contacts with children. But that does not alter the fact that the position of children as a group, in a commercial society, is not wholly advantageous. A commercial society urges its citizens to be responsible for things, but not for people. It is the unquestioned assumption of a mercantile culture that things need and deserve attention, but that people can take care of themselves and no one else has to be, or ought to be, responsible for their welfare. Senator Taft is perhaps the best-known exponent of this viewpoint; but it does not suffer from lack of articulate supporters.

However, even as thoroughgoing a business civilization as that of the United States produces a certain percentage of people who cannot take care of themselves—not, at least, on the terms dictated by the business society. Such people are taken care of by our business society, because it has no choice. It has no traditional sanction—as the agricultural societies of India have—for letting them starve to death, on the ground that they earned their fate in a previous incarnation. Also, these helpless people are consumers, even if they are not producers as that word is understood commercially, and a business society stands in perpetual need of markets. The people who cannot take care of themselves, therefore, are taken care of by a business society; but they are taken care of grudgingly and with constant complaints about how much it costs and how inferior and undesirable such individuals are.

The largest group of people in the United States who cannot take care of themselves is the children. It would be going too far to say that Americans take care of their children grudgingly, since children are much more appealingly helpless than violin players, the aged or the unemployed. But human relationships in the United States are characteristically tense and unrelaxed; and the parent-child relationship is no exception to the general rule. Nor is a nation which has lost 350,000 schoolteachers in a very strong position to argue that its children are the closest thing to its heart.

Schoolteachers have already been mentioned as one of the groups toward whom the overflow, after-business-hours aggression—the Five O'Clock Shadow over the United States—is directed. Schoolteachers, by the very nature of their calling, cannot have market-place qualities. The successful exercise of their profession calls upon them to go squarely across the grain of the American business society. The nature of their job requires that they cultivate the Bankruptcy Qualities—yieldingness, generosity, sympathy, altruism and tenderness. It is easy enough to recall the hostility of American business to the professors in President Roosevelt's Brain Trust. That hostility is an example par excellence of the business society's reaction to people who use their rich, creamy intellects for noncommercial purposes.

The low prestige of schoolteachers in this country stems

from the fact that children are an embarrassment to a business civilization. A business society needs children for the same reason that a nomadic or a pastoral society needs them—to perpetuate itself. Unfortunately, however, children are of no use to a business society until they have almost reached physical maturity. In a religious society, children can be taught about the infant Jesus almost as soon as they can toddle. In an agricultural society, children can feed hens and herd cattle when they are as young as six or seven. In a nomadic society, children can build fires and skin carcasses as soon as their hands have the necessary co-ordination. But it would be dangerous to have kindergartners playing around in a factory, and youngsters of six or seven would be utterly disruptive in an office.

In non-money societies, children begin to participate in the main job of the society at a very early age. They grow up with it, so to speak, and the goals of the society are always an integral part of their lives and memories. But in a business society, an impassable gulf exists between the child and the functioning adult—which is one reason why parenthood in such a society involves a good deal of uncertainty and groping. We are so used to the absence of children in business that it does not strike us as unnatural. But in terms of a society which is to produce contentment and serenity in its citizens, this absence is more than unnatural—it is highly disadvantageous.

Children are basically more responsive to people than to things, since it is people who take care of them and fill their needs. A business society, therefore, always has in its

66

children a large group of individuals who cannot make money and who do not understand (or want to understand) the profit motive. In short, they are subversives, and they belong right at the head of the Attorney General's list.

In describing children as an embarrassment to a business society, the word "embarrassment" is used advisedly. The children of a business society cannot begin to take part in that society until they are adolescent or even older. What is to be done with them in the meantime? It would seem logical to train them to be aggressive, competitive and skeptical, since those are the qualities they will be expected to manifest when they grow up. But there is not room in the American home—or in any kind of home, for that matter—for those single-minded drives which are so much appreciated in corporations and business firms. So the business society does not give its children a formal and conscious training in the market-place qualities, though a considerable measure of those qualities—an ever-increasing measure, these days—filters across the chasm between the child and the functioning adult. In competitive America, for instance, the ironic spectacle can often be observed of children competing to be happy; and Little Johnnie must frequently accept the obligation to be the most "secure" child on the block, or risk seeing his family fall on their sword.

The children of the American business society do not have a formal and conscious education in profit-making behavior, but a formal and conscious education they do have. And this education involves another one of those hidden contradictions which lie at the root of American tension and chronic anxiety. By a sort of historical accident, the children of the United States—while they are waiting to participate in the business society—are given a stylized education in the Judeo-Christian ethic. They are taught that people are more important than property; they are taught the brotherhood of man; they are taught that blessed are the meek; they are taught that no man can serve both God and Mammon. Nothing more unsuitable for their lives as grownups could possibly be devised, but it was either that or nothing. The business society draws a blank when it comes to children.

To refer to the American child's education in the Judeo-Christian ethic—or Christian morality, or the good life—as "stylized" is to suggest that there is a certain absence of passion in this indoctrination. And there is. The United States is a highly verbal society, and the Judeo-Christian ethic is its official morality; but, as I discovered at the Stage Door Canteen, the United States is also a country where "good causes," "crusaders" and "reformers"—American morality in action, that is—are felt to be embarrassing and slightly ridiculous. It might be anticipated, therefore, that the training of American children in the Judeo-Christian ethic would frequently be dilatory and ineffective and would not make a lasting impression on them.

But children are literal-minded and unskeptical. At least, they start out that way. Furthermore, it takes them a long time to learn how to distinguish between fact and fiction. To the child of tender years, a story he reads in a book is just as much a reality as an experience which actually happened to him. He does not differentiate between the two. A child does not decline to believe in the Easter Bunny for the silly, grown-up reason that he happens never to have seen it. If the presents are on the breakfast table Easter Sunday morning, the existence of the Easter Bunny may be taken as proved.

The ethical instruction of American children is sometimes mechanical, but that does not stop the credulous children from trustingly taking the instruction right into their blood streams. The cynical comment that in the United States, the Judeo-Christian ethic is more honored in the breach than in the observance is the comment of an adult, not of a child. Unlike the children of the so-called primitive societies, who participate in the adult world, the child of a business society does not move in business circles. He has no opportunity to see what his spiritual pastors and masters are compelled to do to Christian ethics when they move into the spinning orbit of business and profit.

Gunnar Myrdal called his famous book on race relations *An American Dilemma,* but *the* American dilemma is that conscience is not formed when one is grown up. Conscience is formed in childhood; and the American conscience, shaped unalterably in the American childhood, gives no spiritual sanction to aggression, competitiveness and skepticism. Quite the opposite, in fact. The American conscience, which is no more wholly escapable than childhood itself, sanctions the Bankruptcy Qualities. Hence business activity—no matter how intensive, expansive and apparently successful—cannot produce in the American businessman that automatic, involuntary self-respect which is the basis of real contentment and relaxation.

Happenings abroad have been allowed to obscure the fact that the central problem of our society is not the atom bomb or the Russians, but the ruinous clash of interest between American business and the American family. The Russians are an outside and complicating factor in a situation which, quite in its own right, is painfully reminiscent of the ignorant armies on Mr. Matthew Arnold's darkling plain. Without at all denying the need for the highest intelligence and integrity in handling Russo-American relations, the fact remains that were the entire Slavic Empire to sink into the sea tonight, our basic internal dilemma would be quite unaltered in the morning.

IV

One Nation, Divisible

———

M<small>Y FATHER</small> was a great admirer of American business, and in this he did not differ from many of his countrymen. He also labored under several illusions about American business—and himself in relationship to it—and he never really took its measure. In this, too, he was by no means alone. When my father finished his training as an architect, he worked briefly for a firm of architects and then went into Civil Service. He stayed in the Civil Service for the rest of his working life—thirty-five years—engaged in the not-too-depressing job of building schools for the children of the city of New York. When he retired, in 1937, he was Deputy Superintendent of School Buildings for the metropolis. This was the highest he could go, since the office of Superintendent was a political patronage plum.

My father's job necessitated his having a great deal of contact with building contractors, and these contacts—combined with the fact that he invested his modest savings shrewdly and with skill—gave him an unshakable impression that he knew all about the American business society. And he did know a good deal about American business in its nineteenth-century incarnation. He knew about the kind of business that was still small enough to be, as it was for him, a matter of personal relationships. But the fact that the business society moves—the fact that the small, independent businessmen he knew both socially and professionally were increasingly ingested by large corporate bodies —this fact escaped him.

While my father was working, he received every year at Christmas a collection of expensive and impressive gifts from some of the building firms to whom he let out contracts. Every year he sent them all back—it being his belief that it was not proper or suitable for a man in his position to take them. I once mentioned this in passing to an acquaintance of mine who is highly placed in the public-relations industry. My acquaintance stared at me slack-jawed and said, "You mean he called that *business*!" My father thought that American business was the greatest thing ever invented, and he esteemed it so highly that he went to considerable trouble to have his older daughter trained to take part in it. But he died without ever having perceived the fundamental irony of his position. The irony was, briefly, that for himself, he turned his back on it. When it came to tossing the total of his working years into American business, the old man wasn't having any.

My father was not a businessman, although he thought he was. He was a man with a clear-cut sense of morality and a knack for totting up sums. It is for the privilege of living for a couple of decades in the same house with that clear-cut sense of morality that I am most deeply indebted to him. My father was, like everybody else, an incomplete man and an imperfect man. In some ways, he failed his children. I wish he had been around more when I was a small child. In his old age, I got to know him very well; but it would have been better for both of us if I had had the chance to know him when he was a young man. Nevertheless, in the kind of job he had, he was indirectly a sort of parent or provider for a great many children besides the actual fruit of his loins; and it was the nature of his job which furnished the firm and solid basis of his self-respect. To his great admiration for American business, I did not, fundamentally, pay much attention. My father was like most parents in that what he taught me, he taught me by the way he lived and not by what he said.

In orthodox psychoanalysis, a great deal of emphasis is placed on the analyst as a parent figure; but the reason analysis was of no help to me was that it had no ethical content. The work I did at the Stage Door Canteen was much more therapeutic. The strict Freudians would say that if I gravitate toward morality like filings to a magnet, it is because of my identification with my father. I am not inclined to dispute the statement. I think, however, I would enlarge it. It is my belief that most people, given half a chance, also gravitate toward morality like filings toward a magnet. It is getting half a chance that is the stumbling block.

The mention of stumbling blocks brings us once again —by a natural association of ideas—to American anxiety. Americans themselves freely admit to the tension which pervades their lives. Even the professionally jubilant advertisements allude to it. But before discussing this tension, it is necessary to make a distinction between American unhappiness in particular and human unhappiness in general. American unhappiness is chronic, rather than intermittent. It was not induced exteriorly by famine or high explosives, but seems to spring from somewhere within the American character. And it is inward-turning and passive. The sufferers (another word that is used advisedly) tend generally to seek relief in such things as spectator sports, drinking or looking at television, rather than in reading the classics or taking the five-and-twenty-mile walks with which Mr. Pickwick was accustomed to stabilize himself. From a certain amount of human unhappiness —death, bereavement, illness—we cannot hope to protect our children. Indeed, we do not want to. But it is possible that American unhappiness, if sufficiently dissected and anatomized, need not be passed on in its gnawing entirety to the next generation. Some part of it, at least, might die with us.

The basic cause of American tension is the fact that Americans are taught as children to give and compelled as adults to grab. (The latter activity is sometimes euphemistically described as being "red-blooded," but it does not always feel that way to the people who have to do it.) This about-face in American life is described by the social scientists as a split in the culture. What that technical phrase really means is that there are two Americas. There is the business America, and that is the one which meets the eye. Then there is what might be called the anti-business America, or the child's America, or the family America, or the America of the Judeo-Christian ethic. The anti-business America is more or less subterranean, but that does not mean it cannot make itself felt. These two Americas are a part of each individual's life, just as childhood and adulthood are a part of each individual's life, and these two Americas are mutually exclusive, diametrically opposed in their aims and interests, and completely irreconcilable.

Disunity in American life is often interpreted as meaning that responsible Republican newspapers do not approve of the Republican Senator McCarthy, or that liberal Democrats are appalled by the Southern wing of the party. But the real disunity in American living goes far deeper than politics, although in politics—as in everything else—it finds a blurred and clumsy expression. The real disunity in American life is the disunity *in the individual American*. We are all accustomed to hearing about something which is called "our way of life." Actually, we have not one way of life, but two. We have not one American society, but two. They are in direct contradiction to each other, but we all have to live both of them. Or, to put it more exactly, we have to keep perpetually switching back and forth from one to the other—sometimes almost from minute to minute.

The rift in American life is not a matter of civil war—of the North and the South facing each other across the Mason-Dixon Line. It is not a matter of joining liberal or conservative political parties. If it were, American living would be comparatively simple. The split in American life is a split in the mind and heart of any given American. The trouble is not that we have two conflicting ways of training people, but that any given American is trained in both ways. The trouble is not that we have two contradictory societies, but that those two societies inhabit the same piece of protoplasm—the same hard-pressed chunk of living tissue.

The perpetual dilemma of the American is that if he follows the rules of the business society, his conscience is uneasy and he feels unfulfilled and harassed; but if he follows the rules of the Judeo-Christian ethic, the business society calls him a subversive—which, in its terms, he is—and throws the book at him. The wonder is not that our business society, queen among business societies, is also the most anxiety-ridden. The wonder is that we have been able to maintain even such a perilous balance as we have. If the hackneyed phrase about "our way of life" means anything, it means that the human nervous system is able to absorb an awe-inspiring amount of punishment without retreating into lunacy.

One has but to look, and the split in American life reveals itself in a thousand ways. It shows up in the fact that our political structure is to a large extent a series of "good causes" turned into law, and yet "good causes" in the United States are popularly regarded with skepticism, condescension and defensive amusement. It is a part of the fiction of American life that everybody likes, respects, enjoys and admires business activity. Whereas the fact is that the American not only receives no direct childhood training *for* business—he actually receives a specific childhood training *against* the qualities which furnish the driving-power of business and "success." As a recipe for nervousness, confusion and nameless dissatisfaction, this situation is hard to beat.

It may seem that a contradiction is involved by affirming in Chapter III that the United States is a business society and stating in Chapter IV that the United States is not a single, but two societies existing (or trying to) side by side. However no real contradiction is involved. Of the two American societies, the business society is the dominant one and the most conspicuous one. It sets the hurried tempo of American living and creates the psychological and emotional climate in which we all move. It does this through the communications industry, which is just that—an industry. And not a cottage industry, either, although it sometimes, with demurely downcast lashes, likes to pretend it is.

The American business society, nevertheless, is confronted for all its dominance by a minority problem of which civil rights for Negroes is only one small part. It is haunted, hamstrung and held back by a collection of minorities, numbering in the tens of millions, who are

77

either dubious about the profit motive or (as is more usually the case) indifferent to it. Chiefest among these minorities are the children the business society must have if it is not to die out, and the women who bear and rear them. Also included in this huge concourse of dissidents and revolutionaries—of people who cannot or will not take care of themselves on the basis of every man for himself and devil take the hindmost—are the aged, the artistically talented, the sick, the schoolteachers, the unemployed, nurses, government employees, social workers, unaffluent ministers of God, self-sacrificing doctors and various modest servants of the common good.

In speaking of civil rights for Negroes as only one part of a huge minority problem, I do not at all wish to play down the crucial importance of equality for all races. My daughter, however, is four years old; and it seems to me quite possible that, if God spares her, she may live to see the day when Negro Americans and Caucasian Americans can inhabit the same pleasant suburbs on terms of amiability. Neither she nor anybody, however, will see the day when the business society is able to assimilate its women and children. The most implacable reality of our time is not the hydrogen bomb, but the fact that children need love. And the only place they can get it, in a steady enough supply to be of any use, is from the indigestible legions of the unbusinesslike.

It is of no consequence whether the United States is described as two societies, businesslike and unbusinesslike, or whether it is described as a business society with a permanently insoluble minority problem. What is important is that nobody likes the business society, because it is not a thing anyone *can* like. The business society can be listened to and obeyed without question—and by millions of people, it is. But it cannot command loyalty, as the Judeo-Christian ethic can command loyalty, because—with its basic philosophy of disguised self-seeking—it is unable to return loyalty.

The crucial question about a business society is not how the square pegs get along—the business failures, the creative artists, the "confused liberals." The crucial question about a business society is how the round pegs get along. There are always square pegs in any society, and they always make heavy weather of it. There are neurotic Hopi Indians and paranoic Bantus. The danger sign in the business society, however, is that the round pegs make heavy weather of it, too. If the business society were a fundamentally healthy arrangement—if it were able to sustain and satisfy people in their total personalities and not just as money-makers—that fact would show up in the statistics. If it were humanly possible to *like* the business society, the businessmen would like it. That liking would be reflected in there being much less alcoholism, divorce, suicide, impaired sexuality, psychosomatic illness and nervous collapse in the upper income brackets than in the lower. In a money society, that is what one ought to find.

But one does not find it. American tension is universal and all-inclusive. It cuts across party lines, income lines,

color lines, geographical lines and every known classifica-
tion of the American people. The square pegs are afraid
of the business society—and with reason. It is punitive.
Heretics, rebels, dissidents and people who ask embarrassing questions, it serves up to columnists on the half-shell.
As a rule, and with some notable exceptions, the square
pegs either cower in silence or make unwilling and shame-
faced attempts (like other men, they have dependents) to
appease the business world.

But the square pegs are not important.* It is not fair to
judge a business society except in terms of the businessmen it aspires to, and does, produce. It is not fair to judge
a business society except in terms of the round peg in the
round hole—the businessman in the business society. And
if the square pegs are afraid of the business society, the
round pegs are afraid of finding out they are afraid of it.
The cruel burden of the round pegs is that they can never
rid themselves of the *temptation* to be square pegs. This
is the split personality which a split society—two societies
masquerading as one—inevitably produces.

It is part of the fiction of American life that business is
a very satisfying and rewarding activity. It is a fact of American life that American business has produced in a good
many citizens of the United States a considerable measure
of bitterness, disappointment and disillusion. I cannot
claim to be one of the disillusioned ones, but there were
certainly two things I did not learn in my comprehensive
and well-planned business course. They took me by surprise.

* Save that there are so many of them.

The first was that there was going to be a depression. I was released from the groves of Academe in 1930, and at that time Ph.D.'s from the Harvard School of Business had the jump on me in the coveted chance to get a job emptying wastebaskets. With some brief but scary intervals, I managed to keep working during the lean years; but my first impression of the American business society was not that it callously failed to appreciate sensitive literary folk. When first it dawned upon my ken, American business was having a little trouble absorbing even the unlettered, unlyrical business folk like me. I remember that during the cold winter of 1931, it was my custom to buy an apple every morning on the way to work from one of the unprosperous fellows who sold them in those days. But after a few weeks, the personnel manager asked me not to bring the apple into the office. It was, he said, bad for morale.

A second thing I did not learn in my business course was that if I were going to be a "success"—and in the United States, who wasn't?—I would have to compete with males as a male. From this unequal contest, I shrank. I have the usual American sympathy *for* the underdog, but no particular yearning to *be* one. In addition, my genes, chromosomes and hormones—to which I am pathetically attached—set their faces firmly against any such abdication. My business training and experience proved, eventually, valuable—though not quite in the way my father had anticipated. They gave me a permanent skepticism about the phrase, "confused liberal." In the springtime of my life, I saw so many confused conservatives as to have formed

81

the impression—never since moderated—that confusion is basic and fundamental in American life and not to be laid at the feet of any one school of political thought.

The basis, then, of American tension is the split personality from which we all unavoidably suffer. Two conflicting societies, officially designated as one, inevitably produce human beings who must willy-nilly try to go in two directions at once. The question which naturally arises is how we happen to have gotten into this dilemma in the first place. If we now have two societies, instead of one, it is because the United States has not always been, as it is today, a country organized extensively and intensively for the pursuit of trade, commerce, money and profit.

Until the beginning of the Industrial Revolution, the United States was a predominantly agricultural society. As such, it gave a good deal of leeway and freedom to the ancient and traditional morality which the settlers and colonizers brought over from Europe with them. This does not mean that the early Americans were better people than we are. They were not—as Indians, slaves, indentured servants and certain ill-fated citizens of Salem, Massachusetts, could very well testify. To say that the Judeo-Christian ethic comes down to us from our agricultural past is not to suggest that that past was idyllic and pastoral. On the contrary, it was in many ways harsh and brutal, and very little research is needed to uncover Colonial customs —flogging and the stocks, for instance—which by our standards are needlessly cruel. The early Americans were not better people than we are. There were, however, fewer of

82

them; they were not mechanized; and they lived in an agricultural society. (Despite certain commercial centers on the Eastern seaboard, like Salem and Boston, the prevailing occupation of pre-industrial America was the transformation of the wilderness into tilled land.)

In an agricultural society, the family tends to be larger and more interdependent and close-knit than the family as we know it today; and the other social groups—the church, the city, the town meeting, the market—are smaller and more personal than our social groups. Relationships between human beings are more intimate. In present-day, mass-production America, the opinions we form of our great lovers or our great industrialists are not based on personal contact with them—or even on contact with people who know them well. What we think of our great lovers or our great industrialists is decided for us in the paneled offices of public-relations firms or over the luncheon table in tensely sophisticated restaurants. Practically speaking, the man of distinction in an agricultural or frontier society must try to *be* good; whereas in a business society he need only *appear* to be good. It seems like an easier goal, of course, but it sometimes appears to leave the conquistadores spitting out ashes.

In our inherited morality—and in sharp contrast to the business society—protection of the weak is a cardinal point. In a frontier society, such as ours used to be, protection of the weak is important. It means, in fact, protection of almost everybody, since, confronted by untamed Nature, all men are to some extent feeble and "unbusinesslike."

83

It may seem somewhat startling to mention protection of the weak as having been important on the American frontier, since a good many history books, orators and editorial writers create just the opposite impression. Kit Carson, Daniel Boone, and Lewis and Clarke are often mentioned as the spiritual godfathers in aggression of the modern American businessman. But frontier America was the godfather of business America only in so far as it took away from the aborigines the land which was rightfully theirs. The wagon trains, on the other hand, in which the early Americans went West, and the various "bees" at which they built houses and cleared land for each other were examples of co-operative, not competitive, behavior. The American pioneers had a simple choice—co-operate or die.

American morality, therefore, had a chance to get established in the ante-business United States because in those years of our history protecting the weak was a useful way of behaving. A second reason for the establishment of this morality was that, in pre-business America, people had to be dealt with as individuals, since there was no way of reaching them in the mass. (Not, that is, as we understand reaching people in the mass.) This does not mean that agricultural America, in treating people as individuals, always treated them well. It did not, by a long shot. But it had no way of pressuring or manipulating people, sixteen or eighteen hours a day, to make them behave like part of a market, or part of a labor supply, or part of something called "public opinion." This enforced emphasis on individuality provided a favorable climate for the Judeo-Chris-

84

tian ethic, which views man not as a consumer, but as a total, twenty-four-hour personality.

It is the twenty-four-hour aspect of living which accounts for the fact that Christian morality, before the Industrial Revolution, had a chance to get itself embedded into American tradition and, to some extent, into the Declaration of Independence and the Constitution. In an agricultural or a pioneering society—or even a trading society based on wind and sail—the working day does not end at five o'clock. The distinction between work and non-work is not as painfully sharp as it is in our business society. Home and livelihood, instead of being miles apart both geographically and emotionally, are often combined. Hence the pre-business Americans adopted the Judeo-Christian ethic as the official American morality, not because their Nobility Quotient was higher than ours, but because that ethic fitted into the way they had to live.

It is still our national morality, although the United States is now a business and not an agricultural society. However, so far from dovetailing with the business society and thriving in its climate, it is at loggerheads with business. Why, then, when the United States evolved into a business society, did not that business society develop its own ethic? Because it could not. One needs ethics to live, because living is an around-the-clock proposition, but one does not need ethics to make money. In fact, they are a handicap. The business society is interested in training its citizens to make money, and, in this objective, it is often successful. Many of them do make money, and the ones who do not obligingly regard themselves as failures who have wasted the precious gift of life. But if we are to have a national morality at all—if we are not to descend into a bottomless pit of anarchistic self-seeking—then the only morality available is the leftover morality from our agricultural past. In other words, we are compelled to have not one, but two societies.

If the child of a business society could live in the business world—if it were physically possible for children to start dabbling in business at the age of four—the Judeo-Christian ethic would probably have disappeared from the United States many years ago. However, the American business society would have disappeared with it. Without family life in some more or less stable form, no society can keep going. Fortunately, it is not possible to be an American businessman without first having been a child. Hence, our official national morality has been able to function as a brake on a business society which—for all its very real contribution to the lightening of mankind's burden—has a strong drift toward suicide.

In speaking of ethics and morality, I recall that I have mentioned my father as a man with a clear-cut sense of both. I should not like to give the impression—as to some of my readers, I might—that this meant he was an unlikable person. Indeed, quite the opposite is true. People liked him because they knew where he stood. There was no shabby compromising, no ambiguity and no tattletale gray about him. He was all black and white. In the kind of job he had, he could afford the luxury of being forthright; and he was supremely competent in his job. Since he had nothing to hide and nothing to defend, he was free to be friendly and outgoing to his fellow human beings. Not only was he generous in giving compliments, but—what is rarer—he was poised and dignified about receiving them.

Like all Americans, he lived under tension. His harrowing adolescence had left its mark on him, and he was definitely inclined to irascibility. But although "Civil Service" is usually construed to mean a timorous drudge —burrowing like a mole toward the inglorious haven of a pension—my father was an extremely self-confident person. Oldsters will remember that during World War I, there was such a burst of feeling against the Germans that German music was not played by orchestras, and people whose names had been Schmidt hurriedly changed them to Smith. My father's father was of English ancestry, but his mother was an Austrian; and his mother had given him the Christian name of Reinhold. During the height of the anti-German feeling, a committee of citizens called on my father and suggested that if he wanted them to believe in his patriotism, he would have to change his name from Reinhold to Reginald. My father told them to go jump in a lake; and although the committee had behind them considerable of the popular feeling in our community, they shambled uncertainly out of our house like a flock of sheep. My old man was not the Reginald type.

This does not mean that he was fearless. He knew what it meant to be afraid. He was desperately afraid of poverty and deprivation. He was afraid—until the time came for him to do it—of dying. And one of my most vivid memories, as a small child, is of seeing him go past my bedroom door one night when we had all been awakened by a noise in the cellar. The old man was not approaching the problematical situation below stairs with eagerness and joy. Will power conquered natural prudence; but not, as I could tell from his face, by a handsome margin. (It turned out there was nothing and nobody there, and we never did find out what had disturbed us.) I have seen fear in my father's eyes—and I probably did not see it as often as it was there.

By the Freudian analysts, Reinhold was lightly brushed aside as an anal-erotic; and it is certainly true that he was grimly methodical, compulsively neat and a sufferer from constipation. But that was by no means the whole picture of the man. He would not take presents when he was working, but he felt free to take them upon the occasion of his retiring. And when he retired, he received so many presents that the American Gothic house he bought for his declining years is still cluttered with the tributes—some of them in touchingly bad taste.

I have often wondered about the really surprising outburst of affection and gratitude which my father received at the termination of his working life. I finally concluded that what lay underneath it—aside from his passion and energy and slightly rhetorical Victorian charm—was the fact that he had mastered the fine old art of taking responsibility. He was utterly trustworthy. He knew—without knowing that he knew it—that there are times when you have to do the right thing, no matter what it costs, simply because the right thing has to be done. For this kind of reliability, people are intensely grateful.

My father, though staunchly provincial in his tastes and arbitrary in his morality, was inclined as a general rule to like his fellow man. But Franklin Delano Roosevelt he loathed. Like many other Republicans, he voted for Roosevelt the first time. But my father had had it hard about making a living, and the genial way in which F.D.R. dispensed the public funds caused him almost physical anguish. Since I voted for Roosevelt all along, the relations between me and my father were not always the relations of two fluting, cooing doves. He disliked Heywood Broun, too, and although I never had the privilege of meeting the late, great columnist, my father always referred to him irritably as, "Your friend, Heywood Broun . . ."

However, Reinhold had a clear-cut sense of morality; and what impressed me most about that sense of morality —of what is right and what is wrong, and doing good for others—was the fact that it paid off. He was pleased and surprised by the financial success of my first book. Nevertheless, despite his admiration for American business, he never had the slightest interest in the fast buck. The slow buck was his line of country. It was the second and third books, with their definitely ethical slant, which made him feel that he had reared a child he could afford to respect.

Because of the fashion in which he had instinctively

89

brought up his children, my father never had in his family a Hollywood swimming pool which he could either adjust to or stay away from. That I was able to get to know him well, in the closing decade of his life, was partly due to the fact that he and I were living on approximately the same economic level. He had worked his way up to the middle class, and I had worked my way back down to it. It is a source of great regret to me that I did not get around to parenthood in time for my little girl to have a chance to know him. He had a quality which is, I am afraid, disappearing from the American scene. It is a quality which it would be well worth the trouble to try to recapture. He had style.

When my maternal grandmother was a little girl in Scotland, she used to have to recite a poem which began:

"Satan is glad
When I am bad,

"And hopes that I
With him will lie,

"In fire and chains
And dreadful pains,

"With many more
Who cursed and swore,

"And all who did
What God forbid. . . ."

This formidable nursery rhyme went on for pages and pages, and my grandmother and her brothers and sisters

90

had to repeat it from memory every Sunday, in the intervals between attending three church services and eating scratchy meals of cold food. (The Sabbath could not be defiled by lighting a fire.)

Most people would probably agree that this hair-shirt approach to a somewhat gangsterish Deity scarcely deserves the title of an ethic. The official national morality of the United States of America—the Judeo-Christian ethic, as the phrase is used in this book—means a certain kind of behavior. It means behavior based on the belief that people cannot always take care of themselves, and that they are not necessarily inferior and valueless if they cannot. It describes, for example, the action of a group of high-school teachers—in a town near New York—who opened a teen-age civics club to Negro young people, in spite of the implacable hostility of certain influential groups in the community. Since these teachers had tenure, they could not be dismissed, but they were stripped of all the after-school activities at which they had been accustomed to earn a little money to supplement their meager incomes. It describes the conduct of the young white people who co-operated with the teachers in spite of strong pressure put on them by some of their parents to remain inert and passive.

It describes the doctors who eschew lucrative practices and devote themselves to the crucial, but poorly paid and unappreciated, field of public health. It describes the minister and his wife in Hood River, Oregon, who fought a winning battle to compel the American Legion to put back on its Honor Roll the names of the Japanese-American soldiers who fought in World War II. It describes the men and women who have held themselves responsible for trying to get wages of more than twenty-five cents an hour for Spanish-American agricultural workers. It describes the career of Lillian Smith, who gave the cachet of good breeding to morality in the South. It describes the people who accept the low salaries and near-opprobrium of government service in order to have a sense of contributing to the American nation.

It describes my Uncle Will, who spent fifty years reinvigorating failing Episcopal parishes in upper New York State where "the hungry sheep looked up and were not fed." It describes the social workers who have been fighting for recognition of the eight million healthy Americans who are unemployed because they are over fifty-five years of age. It describes the hardy souls who tried to protect the forests of the Alaskan Indians from the American timber interests. It describes a great many schoolteachers and workers in the P.T.A. It describes the tenacity of Laura Z. Hobson in writing *Gentleman's Agreement*, although the smart money said it was a quixotic project. It describes Miss Frieda Hennock, a member of the Federal Communications Commission, who singlehandedly won twenty-five per cent of television facilities for the education of American children. It describes the Secretary of State who would not turn his back on Alger Hiss. It describes, in short, a great deal of uncelebrated—and sometimes markedly unpopular—American behavior which is nevertheless one half of our divided society.

This book has no villains, but the foregoing examples no doubt illustrate that its heroes (as previously indicated) may not be quite the people the American public has been invited to consider heroic. From the above-mentioned list, one thing is readily apparent, and that is, that the key-stone of the Judeo-Christian ethic is action, not passivity. That ethic—trustingly accepted and never wholly shaken off by the American child—was designed as a guide to actual behavior. It does not mean talk. It does not mean good intentions. It does not mean good will. It does not mean reading newspaper editorials. It does not mean full-page, semi-sacred advertisements which can be taken off the income tax. To define the Judeo-Christian ethic satis-factorily, it is necessary to consider the real nature of an ethic, and the real nature of an ethic is that it does not become an ethic *unless and until it goes into action.*

The business society, like the American ethic, also means action and not passivity. Here, one would think, is ground for some sort of compromise. But no compromise is pos-sible, because two totally different kinds of action are meant. Action, in our traditional morality, is directed to-ward the welfare of others. Action in the business society is directed toward one's own profit. When the Judeo-Christian ethic goes into action in the midst of a business society, it always, ultimately, means money out of some-body's pocket. Out of the stockholder's pocket. Out of the

93

taxpayer's pocket. And money out of pocket in a business society is—for reasons to be discussed in the next chapter —an alarming experience, emotionally.

For this reason, and in spite of the fact that the Judeo-Christian ethic is one of our two American societies, no solution to our split personalities can be looked for in regular attendance at church. The American—wishing to be a decent fellow, but afraid of what will happen to him if he declines to put his whole soul into earning money—sometimes turns with his problem to organized religion. But organized religion, in a dominating business society, can do only one of two things. It can either assure the communicant with uneasy bluster that God Himself likes money —a theory which convinces nobody—or it can give him an apologetic, halfhearted invitation to go out and get himself crucified.

If the American were really to do on Monday what he has been reminded of on Sunday—to sell what he has and give to the poor, for instance—he would lose most, if not all, of his friends and acquire a set of vindictive enemies. Furthermore, his gesture would in all likelihood be wasted. Crucifixion is beyond most people's capacity. It takes a unique personality to make it meaningful, so that the sacrifice does not run uselessly down the drain. The business society can be successfully defied only by people who have no illusions about it and who have something good and solid to take its place. Most Americans are temperamentally unsuited to crucifixion and most Americans, through no fault of their own, have a good many illusions

94

about the business society. Hence, to say that organized religion is of little help to us in our dilemma is only to repeat a point which cannot be too much emphasized—i.e., that the split in our society is not a split between clergy and laity any more than it is a split between conservatives and liberals.

It is a split, produced by contradictory pressures, in the single human being—and the clergy are no more exempt from it than anyone else. To run a church, you need real estate; and to possess real estate in even the most modest way is to operate within point-blank range of the business society. To have a church, you need a congregation; and if the congregation is being urged during every waking hour to make and spend money, you cannot very well tell them, literally, to go to hell and restrict your preaching to cherubim and seraphim.

The Judeo-Christian ethic is not nowadays administered to children in quite the hearty doses in which my contemporaries and I received it thirty or forty years ago. But those people who were instructed in it twenty or thirty or forty years ago are still alive. They are still voting. They are still reading the newspapers. And they are suffering an agony of confusion and bewilderment because the middle-class virtues of honesty, decorum and responsibility are disappearing with what seems like incredible speed.

In a recent profile in *The New Yorker,* President Truman was quoted as saying that the Truman Committee, which was said to have saved the taxpayers fifteen billion dollars, never released anything to the papers until it had been established with certainty that no innocent citizen would be maligned. Any thinking we do on behalf of our children is a waste of their time and ours unless it is done as honestly as possible; and honesty compels us to admit that in the ten years since the Truman Committee, we have had a change of moral climate. Maligning innocent citizens has become an established American institution. False charges are made; false charges are printed in the newspapers; false charges are read by the newspaper readers. Even if nobody believes them—and some people do—they are still there in black and white, a bizarre and tax-free legacy for the adolescents and the young people.

Although they do not phrase it in quite the same way, both the professional philosophers and the man in the street are agreed that the most invulnerable bulwark against Communism is a solvent, self-respecting middle class. The American middle class, however, is at the moment groggy and reeling because its old landmarks of morality have disappeared into a murky gloom labeled, ironically enough, "security." Leaving aside the question of who is going to be safe from what, when Senator McCarthy enjoys no less imposing a sponsor than Senator Taft, a still more urgent question presents itself. At least, it is more urgent to parents. That is the question as to why our traditional notions of ethics and justice and fair play went down with such a splintering, powdery crash under what appeared to be pressure from the Communists.

The answer may very well be that the Communists did not have much to do with it. The answer may possibly be closer at home than we imagine. The answer may lie in the fact that all societies move, and business societies, because of their relentless emphasis on "getting ahead," move very fast. The answer may possibly be found in the fact that "our way of life" is not one way of life, but two. The American ethic and American business have always been diametrically opposed and utterly hostile in their views of life and human nature. However, while we still had some surviving remnants of our agricultural past, it was possible to evade or sidestep the clash between them. The American could get through life somehow—give a little, take a little—without being caught squarely between the upper and the nether millstone.

Economists of every shade and stripe, however, are all agreed that a business society must constantly expand. And the more the business society expands—the more it invades the newspapers with advertising, the home with television and the movies with dehumanized heroines—the closer it comes to a knock-down-and-drag-out fight without official morality. And, as a matter of fact, that is exactly what is happening. What appears—to us who are older, at least—as a horrifying decline of public and private morality is in essence a death struggle between the business and the anti-business America. The real nature of American life, as distinguished from the fictional version of it, can be summed up in a single sentence. The American business society, with its relentless pressure on people to be aggressive, competitive and skeptical, has expanded to the point where it must either wipe out the Judeo-Christian ethic or submit to such drastic modification, in terms of ethics and compassion, that it will scarcely be recognizable.

This book is being written in the hope of evolving some kind of philosophy of parenthood which would make the job of raising a child, in these disturbing times, a little more definite and purposeful. In any such philosophy, the first thing that has to be taken into consideration is the fact that the United States is blanketed with an exceedingly dangerous illusion. That illusion is the idea that the American business society and the American ethic have somehow been harmoniously blended into a single society which we can refer to as "our way of life." No such blending has ever taken place. Nor will it. The American business society has not one enemy, but two—the Communists *and* the Judeo-Christian ethic. With what amounts to a genius for confusion, it treats them both as the same thing.

By lumping its two enemies together as identical, American business is wreaking an immensity of havoc on one of them. The Communists do not suffer when compassionate and ethical behavior is described as "left-wing," "radical," "socialistic" or "Communistic"; but the anti-business America is in a state of rout and panic because anyone who has ever lifted a finger on behalf of the square pegs is in danger of losing his livelihood. The point has been firmly established—not to everybody's satisfaction, but beyond any single man's power to buck it—that having had left-wing sympathies during the Great Depression means a permanent corruption of character.

Under the guise of rooting out corrupt character, the

American business society is rooting out character altogether. This, naturally, cuts the ground right out from under the Judeo-Christian ethic, whose stock in trade is character—and, moreover, character capable of sympathy and of action. Furthermore, what might be called our un-Communist scandals would seem to indicate that the business society is succeeding in its blind but purposeful attempt to wreck the American ethic and to establish the United States on a basis of all-out cynicism. It is anybody's guess whether or not we will be able to contain Communism; but the basketball fixes, the revelations of the Kefauver Committee, and the sale of narcotics to teen-agers indicate with dreadful clarity that we have not been able to contain the profit motive.

This does not mean, however, that the business society is composed of evil men. It is not. The business society is composed of harried protoplasm. That protoplasm manages to struggle through what is called the business day (though not exactly with what William Blake describes as "comfort in morning, joy in the noontide"); but it is caught off base by the fact that there is no such thing as the business night. To this awkward situation, different businessmen react differently. Some of them have nervous breakdowns; some of them muddle bravely along in a sort of partially paralyzed way; and some of them retreat into reckless and destructive cynicism.

It certainly cannot be said that cynicism in the United States is on the wane. The basis of cynicism, however, is not innate evil, but ignorance—sheer, genuine, three-ply,

99

naïve, stumbling, fumbling ignorance. The particular ignorance which is involved in present-day American cynicism is just this: That the profit motive, carried to its
logical conclusion, can end up in nothing but the destruc-
tion of American morality. But when American morality
goes, the American business society goes with it. This,
much more than the Russians, is the taproot of that cold
fear with which every man and woman of us is so horrify-
ingly familiar.

However, there may be, in our present unenviable situation, a silver lining. If there is one, it consists of the
possibility that American business may not have made,
under the surface, as much headway against the American
ethic as at first appears. The business society is not really
equipped for the long pull. It has certain fatal weaknesses.
While it gives the rules for victory—in terms of "getting
ahead"—it provides no armor for defeat. Indeed, as many
a successful businessman has found to his sorrow, it drops
no hint as to what to do with the victory once it has been
attained. If the business society is to survive, the businessman who is its ideal product has to be made of self-reproducing protoplasm. But in his capacity as self-reproducing
protoplasm, the business society wants no part of the businessman. Considered in terms of women, children and the
family, the business society's chances for survival are not
impressive. The Judeo-Christian ethic, on the other hand,
does not need our or anybody's business society for its
continued existence; and the Judeo-Christian ethic will
not touch the profit motive with a twenty-foot pole.

The rift in a split society has to be healed in the area where it originally takes place. And that area is in the mind and heart and feelings of the single American—"businesslike" or "unbusinesslike." We have no handy or convenient factions with which we can associate ourselves. Clergyman and layman, liberal and conservative, businessman and child are all in the same boat—the S.S. Schizophrenia. But in our children, the sentimentalists say, we have a chance to start all over. And we do—provided, of course, that we blaze a trail for them by at least making a stab at starting all over ourselves. In this connection, the first question that needs attention is the issue on which the business society and Christian morality are hopelessly and incurably divided—the question of money.

V

The Eggcup Civilization

———

MY LITTLE GIRL is going to have it repeatedly suggested
to her—by every form of hint, inflection, innuendo
and implication in the language—that money is the Great
Simplifier. Against that treacherous dogma, she will need
a little armor. I cannot provide it for her except out of my
own experience. For me, the money which accrued from
my first book was in a manner of speaking a simon-pure
event. Since I was not in debt and had no dependents, it
provided no exquisite sense of release from pressure. Nor
did it represent the consummation of ambitious strivings.
While I had been reared, like all Americans, to be successful, the goal had been a temperate and middle-class
success and nothing—to use a very much overworked word
—fabulous.

This manna from heaven, consequently, could not have

landed with its lethal kerplunk on anyone less prepared for it. Mine is a plodding rather than a towering intellect, so it took me more time than it should have, perhaps, to find my way around the leafy little bower of greenbacks into which I had tumbled. The first thing I noticed was that the possession of money, in a business society, relieves one of the necessity of ever having to explain one's self. The mere clothes you wear—not to mention the restaurants you eat in or the vacations you take—tell people all they want to know about you. It is a great economy of effort; but the drawback is that explaining one's self to people —especially if the dumb brutes show any sign of catching on—is one of the more entrancing of life's experiences. There is nothing like mink for enforcing anonymity.

A second thing I began to notice—rather more slowly —was the inseparability of money and guilt. Only those rare Americans who were brought up as Druids or taught to worship Pallas Athene have escaped hearing that the rich man has as much chance of getting into heaven as the camel of going through the needle's eye. When I was a child, this stern mandate used to worry me. I wanted to be rich, since it was my understanding that rich people did not have to save for a rainy day or go without things in order to go to college. But I also wanted to go to heaven. When I was a child, however, it was not an immediate problem; and I figured that the powerful grownups probably had an answer to it, since they had an answer to everything else.

But a thing exists, the philosophers tell us, in terms of

its opposite; and the presence of money inevitably suggests the absence of it. It is banal—it is extremely banal—to say, "Why should I be drinking Martinis in Twenty-One when small children are getting rickets from not having orange juice?" It is banal, but it is also inescapable. One can reason, if one wishes, that the adult poor are only getting what they deserve; but that still leaves the unnerving possibility that some day, some way, somehow, one is going to be held responsible for their children. Even when money is deliberately set out for and purposefully earned, the underprivileged children keep rearing their disturbing heads. In our country—all the talk about free enterprise, individual initiative, risk capital and the survival of the fittest to the contrary and notwithstanding—money and guilt are Siamese twins.

While my first book made a good deal of money, it did not make enough for me to live on opulently for the rest of my life. What I had achieved was not money, but the access to money—beach rights on a river of gold. Very few Americans live in the eerie world of permanent wealth so acutely portrayed by Scott Fitzgerald. But a comparatively large number of Americans get the opportunity to dabble in the stream. And for any good, red-blooded citizen of the United States, the beach rights ought to be enough. His own power and drive and energy and American training can be counted upon to do the rest. I had, therefore, the entrée to money. I had a "name" and it could be traded upon. At least, it could if I kept it in the newspapers where people would see it. Also, presumably, I had a tal-

ent—and the fact that it was a hesitant, rather self-indulgent, one-cylinder talent was something I soon learned not
to mention. That was heresy. It did not strike the right
note of cheery self-confidence.

Fourteen years have passed since I woke up one morning
to find myself in the chips. After such a long interval, it is
hard to write about the experience without sounding as
if I were, at the time, both shrewd and composed. As a
matter of fact—and for the benefit of my daughter, who is
supposed to be finding out what her folks were really like,
in their unbelievable youth—I was confused, disoriented
and rudderless. The confusion would have been evident
to any moderately perceptive observer, but moderately
perceptive observers are not what the freshly successful are
usually surrounded with. This is not to say that I was
homeless. It was not that I had no place to go. Quite the
contrary. The Terribly Solvent welcomed me with open
arms. In a business society, the more solvent you are, the
guiltier you have to feel about the shabby, flabby two-year-
olds who are not yet out on a paper route. Hence, new re-
cruits to the Society of People Who May Possibly Be Heels
are accorded a more than royal reception. The saints may
rejoice over a repentant sinner, but it is not a patch on
the rejoicing of sinners upon acquiring a new transgressor.

The Terribly Solvent demanded, naturally, that I
should go on being terribly solvent. Or, to be more exact,
they demanded that I should *want* to go on being terribly
solvent. Because they are not ungenerous people, they
would have forgiven and pitied me if I had tried and

failed. But one, and only one, responsibility was dumped into my lap. I did not have to be beautiful. I did not have to be a clear thinker. I did not have to take an interest in politics. I did not have to be kind to animals. I did not even have to write well. But when it came to maintaining my status as a "success," I had to be in there giving it the old college try. However, like others of my fellow-countrymen who had old-fashioned, non-permissive upbringings, I am somewhat allergic to pressure. It is sometimes enough to be told I have to do something, for me to make up my mind not to do it.

There remained, of course, the More-or-Less Insolvent with whom I had spent my whole life—but I was cut off from them because something had happened to me which they had not experienced. You cannot go around to people who are supporting their aged parents and worrying about shoes for the children and ask them to feel sorry for you because you are a bird in a gilded cage. So, over all, the affluent years of my life were rather more tentative than blissful, and only the wish to shield my daughter from certain prevailing falsities induces me to recall their difficulties. From those difficulties I finally dredged up, after a period of some years, the conviction that there might be something to be said for the Downward Step. I learned—by infinitesimal accretions of knowledge, which were painfully slow in building up—that if my life were truly to belong to me, instead of to a couple of other fellows, I would have to get back to my roots. Instead of divorcing the middle class and leaving it behind me, I would have to return to it. That this conclusion needed quite a bit of ferreting out, in a country geared to getting ahead, goes without saying.

Even in a money society, it is not necessary for the average person to know very much about interlocking directorates; but it is of primary importance to know a little something about interlocking directors. After all, you could so easily turn out to be the mother of one. And it is a curious paradox that in a money society, the one thing nobody meditates about very much is money. (To struggle for money, if you do not have it—or to manipulate money, if you do— is not the same thing as meditating about it.) There is an enormous supply of American books and pamphlets designed to help parents explain sex to their children; but aside from a few superficial notes on weekly allowances, very little has been written for mothers and fathers on what should be their conscious attitude about money, business and homo sapiens. I have mentioned certain prevailing falsities in our money society which I should like to see my daughter side-step—notably the careless assumption that money is the Great Simplifier—but it would perhaps be more scientifically accurate to describe these beliefs, not as falsities, but as folklore.

Folklore is a collection of ridiculous notions held by other people, but not by you and me. Actually—although it seems hard to believe at first glance—the business-dominated country in which we live is a teeming hive of folklore about money; and this folklore, dispassionately considered, is just as quaint as anything Scots Highlanders believe about ghosts. Take, for example, the American legend of the Cosy Corporations. No literate American can get very far away from full-page ads and planted magazine articles in which one or another of our giant industrial empires is described as a great, lumbering, affectionate Newfoundland dog panting to lick the face of the beloved American consumer. Friendly General Motors. Likable G.E. Serious-minded U.S. Steel. Jolly good fellows, all of them.

The superstition is firmly established, in the United States, that the American citizen lives like a fluffy chick under the brooding, maternal wing of billion-dollar corporations. The chill and nonmythical reality, however, is that our Big Businesses have no personalities of their own, but are simply random collections of human beings who have been informally but very thoroughly trained to be— between the hours of nine and five—aggressive, competitive and skeptical in the pursuit of money. No such collection of human beings is, or ever could be, any cosier than a hanging judge.

Another well-established bit of American financial folk-lore is the idea that the small, independent businessman has what comes close to being the ideal way of life. In reality, the small, independent businessman is disappearing from the economic scene, except for a worried few whom the Cosy Corporations have not yet, in sheer impersonal momentum, got around to bankrupting. And were the American human being to acquire a small, independent business, could he—product of the Upward Step as he is—

be content to keep it small? Or, were he himself content, would not his wife, his parents, his children, his neighbors, his relatives, his friends, his customers and his bankers regard him as lazy? Two factors make the small, independent businessman increasingly a folk myth instead of a reality. One is external—the trend of our business enterprises to be organized in ever fewer and ever larger empires. The other is internal—the fear of being punished for not "getting ahead."

It is nevertheless easy to see why the idea of the small, independent businessman has such appeal. He seems to represent a healing of the split society. He seems to combine, in his single person, both the admirable mercilessness of business and the compassion and unstudied friendliness of the Judeo-Christian ethic. However, the advertisers and opinion-makers who keep the small, independent businessman so constantly in our mind's eye are not really doing us a service. It is not good for people to have perpetually before them, as a possible reality, a dream which has fewer and fewer chances of ever coming true. We have, to be sure, plenty of small businessmen—as the Cosy Corporations frequently point out in their advertising. But they are not independent. They are in hock. A man's home may be his castle, but his liquor store or his filling station is not. A sub-contractor is not, by any stretch of the imagination, a small, independent businessman.

At first blush, it is hard to grasp the fact that anything so infinitely complex, both financially and mechanically, as our movie industry, our advertising industry, our public-relations industry, our newspapers and our radio-television chains should be engaged in the simple, tribal operation of disseminating myths—differing only in the size of their audience from a medicine man in central Brazil. But reduced to their basic function, that is what they do. The fundamental myth, of course—the one on which all the others depend—is the primitive, pathetic American belief in the magical power of money. Not that one ever finds an average, decent American who actually says he believes money and the things it can buy make people feel better. He actually says just the opposite. But we have all become sufficiently expert in parlor psychoanalysis to know that when you want to find out what people believe, you look at what they do instead of listening to what they say. If Americans did not believe in the healing power of money, they would not spend so much of it. They would stuff it away in an old sock, like the French peasants—sturdy materialists, too, but in their own way.

Since we all have—at least, to a certain extent—this belief in money as God's Trouble-shooter, we all know how deeply ingrained the feeling is in our personalities and how hard it is to shake off, except in momentary flashes of insight. The truth, however, actually does set people free —in so far as they can lay hold of it. Ours is a money society, as everyone freely admits, and a money society inevitably raises, but does not answer, certain haunting and spectral questions. How much money is enough? How much money does a person need? Or, to phrase the questions so that there will be some chance of arriving at an answer, How much money does a person need, considered simply as protoplasm which must be fed, sheltered and clothed? How much money, on the other hand, does a person need as a "successful" member of the dominant, conspicuous, inescapable and constantly expanding business society? The two questions do not, obviously, have the same answer.

Night and day and around the clock, the communications industry pours out its ceaseless message that people can be made "happier" by money and the things that money can buy. The word "folklore"—with its connotation of childlike credulousness—may seem an odd one to use in connection with a business society which prides itself on its practicality. It is, however, clear to all but the dullest intellect that one cannot increase the caloric content of an egg by eating it from an expensive eggcup. And yet in the world as we know it—and as our children must come to know it—"hardheaded reality" is supposed to be represented by the price tag on the eggcup and not by the relationship between nourishing egg and eager, appreciative stomach.

In a previous chapter, mention has been made of the fact that there are certain widely held American beliefs about money which her father and I would like to see our daughter take with a grain of salt. One of the most generally accepted of these beliefs is the notion that the American business society, revolving on its axis of money, is "realistic." Actually, in terms of human flesh and human contentment, "realistic" is just exactly what the American

111

business society is *not*. If there is any sort of answer to the problem of American chronic unhappiness, that answer begins with a firm, unshakable grasp of the fact that the American business society is based upon an illusion.

This illusion is the belief that money and the things it can buy will make people feel better—that money enables people to escape pain, insures them against criticism, makes them more self-confident and authoritative and less prone to self-mistrust and feelings of inferiority. The business society's illusion about the power of money takes tangible form in the Bath of Perfection in which we are all unavoidably immersed—in the perfect teeth, perfect bosoms, perfect young women, perfect romances, perfect clothes, perfect automobiles, perfect medicines, perfect food and perfect furniture which assault our eyes and ears all day and every day and to which we have become so accustomed as not to recognize the inherent menace of their unnaturalness.

It is easy enough to spot an hallucination in a single person. If a man tells us he is Napoleon, we have no trouble in classifying him as demented. But a mass illusion, accepted unthinkingly and without question by millions and millions of people, appears at first glance to have authority and not to be an illusion at all. And, as a matter of fact, all tribes, groups, societies and commonwealths are based to a certain extent on mass illusions—whether those illusions are concerned with totem poles, the spirits of the dead, dryads or dressing for dinner in the jungle. It is therefore no particular discredit to our or the other business societies to say that they are based on an illusion about money. What counts, rather, is whether the mass illusion is practical and workable in terms of human flesh and the human need for a measure of contentment now and then.

The illusion upon which our dominating business society is based—the illusion that money and the things it can buy will make people feel better—is not practical and not workable. If it were, the people in the upper income brackets would be distinguished for being much more contented, fearless, self-respecting and emotionally well-balanced than their less fortunate brethren. But they are not. American chronic unhappiness is no respecter of incomes.

It is hard for Americans to think of themselves as living in a society, since the American business society is never referred to as a society, but simply as Business, with a capital B, as if it were some sort of unusually good-looking and remarkably powerful Greek goddess. Business-with-a-capital-B, however, is nothing more than the unthinking activity of specially conditioned human beings who are doing what they have been told to do. Americans live in a society, a predominantly business society, and What Every Parent Should Know About Business can be telescoped into a remarkably small space. What Every Parent Should Know About Business is that the American business society —for all its unique contribution toward freedom from drudgery—is not "practical" and not "hardheaded" and not "realistic," but illusionary. And unworkably illusionary, at that.

The "reality" is the egg. The "reality" is Nature's divine and comforting miracle of the human alimentary system. The eggcup, to which our attention is so persistently and unremittingly directed, is the fantasy. It is, to be sure, a magnificently well-organized fantasy. In fact, American business—with its torrents of advertising and of entertainment which is really no more than implied advertising *—could quite accurately be described as an Eggcup Civilization. But in terms of children, who are not in business and who need love, the eggcup is nevertheless not the reality. The eggcup is the fantasy.

In trying to work out a philosophy which might remove some of the groping and bewilderment from the task of parenthood, it must be accepted as a First Principle—and never for a moment forgotten—that a thing is not necessarily true just because a great many people think it is. Fifty million Frenchmen may, conceivably, err. And when they do, they pay for it. Nothing is more comfortably intimate, temporarily, than to go along with the crowd and to accept as truth what everybody agrees is the truth. But such good-natured compliance cannot always be relied upon to pay off.

The present writer is a suburban housewife with no claim to intellectual distinction beyond the fact of having predicted, four weeks before the 1948 election, that Harry S. Truman would win. Only my legal matrimonial mate was kind enough not to laugh. Before the election, I was

---

* Neither the movies nor the comics carry a line of advertising, but both of them function as a sort of permanent advertising for uplift brassières.

regarded as a promising candidate for a pre-frontal lobotomy; afterwards, the prediction was described as "feminine intuition." But it was quite clearly observable—in fact, several political pundits commented on it at the time —that the President was campaigning with his whole personality, whereas his opponent was offering the electorate only a parched segment of himself.

American voters being as humanly emotional and responsive as any other set of people in the world, it is a fairly safe bet that in an American election, you can beat a total personality with a stronger total personality—Senator Taft, for instance, also campaigned with his whole personality in 1950—but you cannot beat a total personality with a half-personality. There was an additional factor, too, in the President's victory, about which your correspondent may very well have been intuitive rather than intelligent. That factor is that the American population—harassed, besieged, clamored at, exhorted, guided, directed and intruded upon by the communications industry—can be relied on just in the nature of things to have occasional shuddering, convulsive rebellions against it.

It is a First Principle of parenthood, then, not to accept things as true just because a great many people think they are true. Nevertheless, the widely held American belief that money means "happiness" has a certain surface appearance of truth; and there is every excuse in the world for the most intelligent American to feel that when he has got hold of money, he has got hold of "reality." Americans actually can be made to feel better by acquiring money.

115

They can purchase immunity to criticism. They can buy, along with the Cadillac and the deep freeze, the respect, admiration and half-throttled envy of their fellow citizens. They can duck out from under the unnerving responsibilities of parenthood and leave those responsibilities in the hands of well-trained hirelings. They can run away from themselves in travel. They can evade the laws which crash punitively down on the financially defenseless. They can even, if they are sufficiently in command of this world's goods, make laws. It is a fact beyond dispute that in the United States as it is currently organized, the acquisition of money does, momentarily, make people feel better.

But the deadly parallel is that it is equally indisputable that an alcoholic is made to feel better by his first drink. Alcohol is a food, and a celestially quick-acting food, at that. It is not the food to which the human body responds most gratefully or most gracefully; but that it is nourishment of a sort, no moderately well-informed person is prepared to deny. In a split society, dominated outwardly by its business half, money is nourishing to the spirit in the same way alcohol is to the body. In fact, as some of our novelists have already pointed out, we have developed what might be called the business alcoholic—the man who in his heart does not like business and what it does to him any more than the alcoholic likes liquor and what it does to him, but who is caught in the same kind of trap. For that matter, it is an even worse trap. The drinking alcoholic can at least count upon an occasional sympathetic magazine article describing him as the victim of a disease. The

116

business alcoholic must try to regard himself as a conqueror, however inaccurate he knows the term to be, and he must keep his troubles to himself.

If further evidence is needed that a split society inevitably produces split personalities, one has only to consider that most American businessmen are also American parents—and are thus, although nobody ever tells them so, the innocent architects of some of their own parental dilemmas. The books on child-rearing tell us in a mighty chorus that the good parent relaxes and enjoys his children. But what do the businessmen say when they are talking to each other?

ONE THING NO EXECUTIVE CAN AFFORD TO DO

No executive can afford to stand still.

That is the unpardonable sin in American business. The pace is too fast, competition too keen, to permit any lagging. The man who falls behind is out of the race.

To get ahead and stay ahead, today's executive must keep abreast of the times. He must be informed of the modern management methods employed by successful, progressive companies.

Every alert executive realizes this.

That is why so many top management men are according so prompt and enthusiastic a reception to the new Funk & Wagnalls Reading Course in Executive Technique.*

* Adv.—New York Times Book Review.

117

The books on child-rearing do not tell us how the good parent is to cope with the fact that, in the business society, it is against the law to relax. To relax is to have your job snatched out from under you by some clambering upstart who is tense as a strung bow.

The split personality is always unconsciously trying to heal itself—trying to close the gap. Protection of the weak being inseparable from parenthood, and the United States being predominantly a money society, it is natural for many American parents to assume without thinking about it that they need money for their children, and to mention their children as the reason why they take part in what everybody agrees is a rat race. Making money for one's children—in the strenuous world of aggression, competitiveness and skepticism—is generally referred to as "giving them advantages." Children, however, do not need "advantages." Children need love, and people do not strain after "success" for the sake of their children. The children are just an excuse—albeit an unconscious one. People strain after "success" because they have been taught to make the Upward Step. They strain after "success," not because they have children, but because they have had parents. Childless people are not distinguished, as a group, for being less keen on getting ahead than parents.

No consideration of present-day American children can be very helpful which leaves out of the picture the people who once were children in the United States. We must not let the Upward Step mislead us. What happens to our children is very closely linked up to what happened to us, the adults, when we were children. The disastrous weakness of a business society is that children cannot move in the business world, so that there is always a fence between the child and the functioning adult. What is even worse, there is always a fence between the functioning adult and the child within him—which is another way of describing the American split personality.

Children are indifferent to the profit motive. Grownups are not. Or, at least, we have the word of the American press that grownups, so far from being indifferent to the profit motive, are inspired by it to all their most admirable behavior. Without at all conceding that the profit motive is as universal as the newspapers claim, it is nevertheless true that many Americans are the victims of a blind, compulsive need for money which exceeds by many hundreds or thousands of times their simple protoplasmic requirements for food and shelter. The word "victims" is an important one. All the stock, familiar phrases about individual initiative and free enterprise do not successfully conceal—although they are meant to—the fact that the enterprising American is not usually free to make a deliberate choice between being enterprising or not enterprising about money. He is pressured into his initiative by the threat of punishment and the promise of reward. Enterprise it certainly is, but it would not look like freedom to the Prisoner of Chillon.

American babies, kicking and squirming in their bassinets, have no thoughts or feelings at all about money. Twenty years later—often in a much shorter time—they have acquired, most of them, a very clearly defined attitude about money. This attitude can be summed up in three words. They trust it. They respect—without being aware of the respect—the people who have either inherited or earned it in large quantities. They are inclined to be contemptuous—again unconsciously—of the people who have not been able to earn it. For the people who could have earned it, but chose to do something else, they have a feeling akin to horror. If any doubting Thomas is skeptical about the fact that the American population is both frightened and angered by people who turn their backs on a money-making potential, he has only to try it and see.

Between the American baby's indifference to money and the American adult's reliance on it, what intervenes? In teaching a young person to drive a car, it is necessary to be specific. Similarly, children do not learn arithmetic by hearing the grownups talking about it. But what American children learn about money—what we ourselves learned about it, when we were children—is not the result of specific instruction. Nobody, now or formerly, takes American children by their infant lapels and tells them to go out after the fast buck. Nobody teaches them to make just-barely-legal "deals" the way Fagin taught his charges to pick pockets.

Children, as everyone knows from having been a child, are much more sensitive to inflections and much more perceptive about behavior than their dulled and battle-weary seniors. American children, past and present, learn to have faith in money from hearing the grownups talking about it to each other and from observing the behavior of grownups toward people who have money (or the prospect of it) and toward people who have not. American children learn about money from hearing the grownups pardon the unpardonable and forgive the unforgivable by saying, "But you've got to admit, he makes money." Children learn about money both from the grownups they know and from the grownups with whom they are not personally acquainted—notably, today, the grownups who shape policy in the communications industry. They learn, also, as much from omission as from commission. They learn as much from what is not on radio or television as from what is there. If there is one thing in the world about which children are experts, it is sincerity. The occasional isolated— and castrated—exhortations to virtue from the communications industry are correctly assessed by children as not having been torn raw and bleeding from the hearts of the exhorters.

A specific training can be successfully rebelled against and shaken off. Children can, and often do, promptly and completely forget all their arithmetic the moment the last exam is passed. But the training American children receive about money is nonspecific, atmospheric, subtle, intangible and pervasive. It is therefore supremely difficult for the adult American to free himself of it. We can all of us remember without too much difficulty when and under what circumstances we learned arithmetic. Very few of us can point to the day and the hour when we first began to learn that Americans get punished for not having money. Very few of us can remember the exact moment when we began to be afraid of not having money. Afraid in terms of our physical wants. Afraid of being old and ill and alone in a nonwelfare state. And equally afraid—every bit as much afraid—in terms of our need for recognition and for belonging.

A split society is a complex society. Wearisomely complex. The complexity of life in the United States stems from the complexity of the people in the United States and not, as is often suggested, from the complexity of the machines. The American business society is owned and operated by businessmen who spent a good many years being children before they got to be businessmen. In that prebusiness period, they had a specific training in the Judeo-Christian ethic and an atmospheric training in business behavior. The business society does not, therefore, come right out and say in so many words that money is everything. In fact, every year at commencement time, when the pillars of the business society get honorary degrees, they make a special point of telling the fledgling graduates that money is not everything. What the business society actually says to the young people is that, while money is not everything, money comes first. First you make your pile, and after that sacred obligation has been discharged, you are at liberty to go in for hobbies, leisure, philanthropy, psychoanalysis, politics, religion, art or getting to know your children.

The only trouble with this arrangement is that, in terms

of peace of mind, it will not work. When money comes first, it stays first—all good intentions notwithstanding. The business society pays unfailing lip service to the official ethic. It has to, because the customers were brought up on it. The business society even permits the businessman to throw an occasional sop to that morality, provided he does not let the sop-throwing interfere with the serious business of financial advancement. But—and here is the very crux and kernel of American chronic unhappiness—the Judeo-Christian ethic is, like the law, a jealous mistress. One can no more pay mere lip service to it, and get results, than one can pay mere lip service to business, and get results. Both of our two societies demand all or nothing.

Everyone knows what is meant by getting results in the business world. But what is meant by getting results in terms of the Judeo-Christian ethic? This question can best be answered by pointing out that the purpose of that ethic is to support people. This makes it exactly the opposite of the business society, whose purpose is to make money out of people. The purpose of the American ethic is to give help—to comfort people when they are alone, to support them against uncomprehending criticism, and to give meaning to their lives. The great disadvantage of being in a rat race is that it is humiliating. The competitors in a rat race are, by definition, rodents. It is the purpose of Christian morality to keep people out of rat races, and to give them the feeling of being dignified human beings with a personal responsibility for choosing between good and evil.

We may all certainly be excused for thinking of the Judeo-Christian ethic as a fancy accessory, like the overdrive on an automobile, to the "realistic" pursuit of money. That is the way it is always presented to us. But there is absolutely no way out of our present confusion save by accepting the fact that our traditional national morality is not an overdrive on the business society, but a way of life in itself. A way of life has to be lived. It does, at any rate, if it is going to pay off in terms of being a human being and not a badgered animal. Such a way of life has to be lived, furthermore, during the best years of one's earthly span, and not during the tag end left over after the annuities have been corralled. The purpose of our ethic is to protect people, but there is one form of protection which it adamantly withholds. It does not protect the strivers after money, successful or unsuccessful, from the consequences of striving after money. There are certain groups of people in the American population for whom American ethics actually do pay off, but as they do not make much money, they will be discussed in a subsequent chapter. They do not belong in this one.

Every human being has his own particular way of showing off. My particular way is to set up a bridge table and a typewriter in the engaging privacy of my bedroom, and see what I can do with the lessons in paragraph structure which intermittently starred my well-spent youth. The stage, the lecture platform or even the commanding position by the fireplace in a Sir Frederick Lonsdale drawing room have never constituted my particular outlet for what can be called either exhibitionism or self-expression. However, after I had on the record a published work on race relations, I taught myself—or rather, my husband taught me—to give a passable lecture on the thorny subject of Negroes and Caucasians in the United States of America. It was the Deity's obvious and visible intention that I should communicate with my fellow men through the written rather than the spoken word; but there exists among white Americans a great craving for affirmation and reassurance in their tentative efforts to set things right vis-à-vis the Negro Americans.

At these lectures, there was almost always some well-meaning soul who had brought along a rich old uncle—the uncle being rich by virtue of owning Negro tenements in Miami. The well-meaning souls always hoped that Uncle —having been given the straight dope on race relations by the speaker of the evening—would see the error of his ways and go in for slum clearance. So far as I know, Uncle never did, although I met him often. But in the question-and-answer periods which usually followed these lectures, the inevitable Uncle always made a point which is germane to the whole subject of parenthood. He always made the point that segregation of Negroes does not need our attention, since the coming generation—who will be much more enlightened and advanced than we are—can be relied upon to straighten out the matter with far less trouble than it would be for us.

This, of course, is cold comfort to the people who are being Jim-Crowed at the present moment. It is also nonsense. Our children will be as courageous as we are—

neither much more nor much less—because we are the only people from whom they can learn courage. If young people learn to be courageous, they learn it from associating with courageous grownups. Providence, in its wisdom, does not select one generation rather than another to be especially kind to. If the next generation of American children escapes the rat-race destiny and knows enough to look at the egg instead of the eggcup, it will only be because we, the adults, set their feet in that path and help to keep them there.

All normal human parents have the wish to do something kind and fruitful and constructive for their children. In our country, this wish has, up to now, taken the form of the Upward Step—of launching the children into American life on a higher rung of the financial ladder than the one the parents started on. But we are beginning to have the painful fact borne in on us that the Upward Step is not the answer to life. It undeniably produces an ever higher standard of living, physically, but it separates parent from child. It deprives children of that understanding of their parents as human beings which the children need to have if they are to arrive at self-knowledge and contentment. The Upward Step makes people lonely. It cuts them off, to a certain extent, from the most comforting and stabilizing of all sensations—the feeling of the continuity of life as it flows through the generations.

The kindest, most fruitful and most constructive thing which can be done for American children is to refrain from passing on to them, uncritically and unquestioningly, the tribal superstitions of the money society—the illusion that the American business society is "realistic," and the conviction that the more money people have, the better they will feel. More than any amount of "advantages," the American child needs parents who have correctly appraised the real situation in the United States—the real situation being that in our country, money, while not everything, comes first. That is to say, the businessman in his role of businessman is more important than the businessman in his role of parent. A more ridiculous setup it would be hard to imagine, since the human race can get along without business, and often does, but it cannot get along without parents and children. Having recognized, then, that American life is not so much complex as upside down, it is time to return to the disturbing question which a money society raises, but does not answer—to wit, How much money is enough?

VI

Money Is a Bandage

IT WAS with something of a start that I realized—a couple of months ago—that for the last ten years, my standard of living has been steadily declining. At least, that is one way of putting it. Another way would be to say that, although I was not aware of the process, I have been for the past decade consistently shedding material possessions and social entanglements and reverting to the austerity of my childhood. Ten years ago, I was a great girl for having things nice. In the United States, having things nice is a national pastime, like baseball, and I was devoted to it heart and soul. I had people in to dinner, and I had a maid to cook the dinner. The hostess may not have been a miracle of emotional stability, but the tablecloth blended with the carpet and the glassware was not infelicitous in design.

My Spartan upbringing has always prevented me from going really hog-wild about clothes; but ten years ago, the ones I had were good, and I took meticulous care of them. Nor did it occur to me at that time that I could attend a social gathering without pancake make-up, lipstick, rouge, eyebrow pencil, eye-shadow and mascara doing their humble best for my physiognomy. At the present time, my husband and my daughter and I occupy a six-room house; but as we moved into it from a three-room apartment, and as it took every penny we could raise just to make the down payment, the ménage does not suggest the Petit Trianon. The first floor has curtains and enough furniture so that visitors are not startled, but the second floor looks as if we were just getting ready for a barn dance. In the foreseeable future, there is no possibility that it will ever look otherwise. As for your correspondent, the gracious chatelaine of this moated grange, she wears cotton shirts and blue jeans to everything but weddings, christenings and funerals.

Of course, the advent of my daughter had a little something to do with my deserting from the bright banner of *Vogue* and *House Beautiful*. But actually, the process started before that, and my husband was an inadvertent contributor. My little girl's father has many beautiful and endearing qualities, but tidiness is not one of them. After a period of considerable strain, I reached a point in my life where I could see that I had to make an interesting choice. I would either have to give up the unfailing orderliness which I took over from my father, or I would have to give up being married. I could not have them both. By, paradoxically enough, the exercise of a great deal of self-control, I managed to shed some of my perfectionism. I will never, of course, reach the glorious heights of careless-ness upon which my spouse lives. While I am now able to drop a book or a coat on the floor, I will never—to my dy-ing day—be able to do what my husband does. I will never be able to tread on it on my way out of the room.

Since this chapter is to deal, in the fullness of time, with money and the question of how much money is enough, it might be added that another element of my retreat from having things nice was economic. There is a good deal of difference between my present frugality and the frugality my mother and father exercised when I was young. My parents were saving money to send their two daughters to college and to enable them—my folks, that is—to have an independent old age. My husband and I are, like many of our fellow countrymen, not saving any money at all. It takes all we can earn, in our honorable but unresplendent professions, to give our little girl approximately the amount of trees, space and fresh air we had when we were small—as well as access to a public-school system approxi-mately as good as the ones we attended.

Lest this sound like self-pity, it should quickly be added that circumstances have changed a good deal since my parents made their regular monthly deposits in the savings bank. A college education for our daughter is not quite the bright, definite and glorious goal for my husband and me that it was for both our sets of parents. For one thing—as has already been noted—the middle class is now pretty generally agreed that these present years of my daughter's life are more important to her character and happiness than the four years she spends between seventeen and twenty-one. These, therefore, are obviously the years on which to spend the money.

But how much money? How much money is enough? Perhaps the simplest approach to this query is to begin with human protoplasm. It is a fact beyond dispute that all Americans are made of protoplasm; and it is equally indisputable that human flesh is a rather tyrannical agency. There is a definite limit to how much food it can take in. It provides only a relatively small area upon which to drape even the most expensive clothes. It refuses to be any less sleepless or infirm in a twenty-room house than it is in a two-room apartment. And after an arbitrarily determined stay upon this planet, it disappears. If the needs of flesh and blood were all that had to be considered, a good many Americans who are now tense and strained about their incomes could afford to stop worrying. The money in a money society, therefore—the money so compulsively dreamed of, so tensely earned and so freely spent—must be serving some further purpose, for a great many people, than the mere maintenance of physical health.

This further purpose can be quickly enough described. In a business society, it is the function of money to take the place of affection. With the family on iron rations, human beings—a category which includes the businessman himself —cannot get from their parents, their children, their relatives, their neighbors, their friends, their co-workers or their fellow voters the warmth and security which all human beings absolutely must have. Once in a while, at any rate. Hence the people in a business society—for all the human dignity of their advanced medicine and their labor-saving devices—are under the painful necessity of trying to live in a prevailingly suspicious, cynical and unaffectionate atmosphere. In this withering situation, money—whether real, potential or only impotently dreamed of—is supposed to provide the protection and the emotional security which the beleaguered and discredited family cannot supply.

All writers are accustomed to being asked, once in a while, where they get the ideas for their work. The idea for this book—the little germ or kernel which started it off —came to me some years ago when I was writing about Negro-white relations and doing some reading on the subject to check my facts and figures. At that time it began to seem to me that discrimination against Negroes is only one part of a national pattern of underdeveloped affection; and that the punitive behavior of whites toward Negroes has its roots in the punitive behavior of whites toward other whites.

It should here be stated that this discussion of how much money is enough is not to be interpreted as an attack on the "haves" and a glorification of the "have-nots." I should be dismayed if this book were construed as a defense of the liberal tradition, since, in this writer's view, the liberal tradition does not need any defense. It just needs liberals. Rather, this is a conservative book, in the dictionary sense of the word "conservative"—meaning to save or preserve.

At this juncture, it would perhaps be wise to restate the purpose of the family. The family's job is to provide a clearly understood, workable relationship between the older people in a society and the younger ones who will eventually take their places. Children, however, are indifferent to profits and finance and they need affection, not money or "advantages." In a society based on profit-making, therefore, there can obviously be no clearly understood relationship between the older people and the younger ones. In such a society, the family must necessarily do its job superficially, intermittently, unsatisfactorily and with a great deal of strain, anxiety and tension.

Hence, the division of Americans into "haves" and "have-nots" is artificial and meaningless. The poor can be, and often are, just as effectively alienated from the Bankruptcy Qualities as the rich; and the mere absence of money is not in itself a sign of wholesome living. There is no basic difference between a man who is straining—for reasons he has never asked himself—to build a drygoods empire and a man who is straining to keep up the payments on a television set which he bought because everybody else has one. One man is a so-called producer and the other is a so-called consumer, but they are both helpless and uneasy drifters on the cold and uncongenial tide of American business.

Some Americans—through sheer good luck, not personal merit—happen to move more within the orbit of the Judeo-Christian ethic than within the orbit of American business.

Such people tend to choose, consciously or unconsciously, the kind of life work like schoolteaching, government service or motherhood where the only possibility of advancement is emotional and spiritual, not financial. I have spoken of such people as being fortunate, but it is a very modest kind of good fortune. The unbusinesslike Americans are always on the receiving end of the business society's hostility and contempt; and while their choice of jobs indicates that they do not aspire to more money than protoplasm needs, they must sometimes get along with a little bit less. They must also manage to get along with virtually no prestige, applause or recognition.

If one takes the customary path and divides Americans into "haves" and "have-nots," then it is easy to find pure types. If, on the other hand, one divides them more realistically into people who have been prevailingly influenced by business or prevailingly influenced by the American ethic, then it is impossible to find any pure types. A really pure type of the American businessman would have to be born at the age of eighteen. A really pure type of the American businessman would have to have no memory of a time when he was weak, helpless, dependent and in need of affection. On the other hand—ethic or no ethic—the piece of flesh and blood does not exist which can live in the middle of a business society and remain totally unaffected by its attitude toward money and toward the purchase of those charming or uncharming perishables which moth and rust do corrupt and thieves break in and steal.

Despite my own accession to unexpected cash—which

forced me to do a little laboratory work on money and its connection with the sense of well-being—I seldom have a fit of gloom or depression without feeling that if I could just go out and distribute some coin of the realm, my spirits would lighten. If I could buy a lamp for my little girl's room, or purchase, after exquisite deliberation, an ornament for the dining room whatnot, the sense of worthlessness would be replaced by a sense of worth and the sense of powerlessness by a sense of power. Since there is very little room in our budget—it being a characteristic of budgets not to have much room—for the Cure of Despondency by Expenditure, I must either sweat out my dejection or get it lightened, free of cost, by other human beings. (As we all know, this last is a risky procedure.) But the first impulsive, unreasoned (and socially conditioned) reaction is always there—that if I could just go out and acquire something, I would feel better.

This writer has been identified as conservative, in the dictionary sense of conservative as saving and preserving. Within the past few years, there have been several books —and they have enjoyed a good deal of popularity—pointing out that our natural resources of forest, soil and water are being recklessly wasted and destroyed owing to certain groups of human beings who are somewhat elusively identified as "the timber interests" and "the public-utility interests." By people who have looked into it and ought to know, we are told that the conservation of our natural resources calls for certain "socialistic" institutions like a Missouri Valley Authority and a Columbia River Authority. The establishment of these preservative institutions has been blocked by various influential stockholders who do not want to go through the emotionally painful experience of taking less profit. Warmhearted but hot-tempered liberals point out with considerable asperity that these influential, stockholding human beings and their managerial grand viziers live considerably above the subsistence level; and thus their motives can only be ascribed to plain greed. But this is inaccurate. The inability to take less profit does not come from greed. It comes from need. In a business society, the emotional economy is an economy of scarcity.

Children need affection. Love, and not money, is what children try to get. And since there is always continuity in any person's life, no grownup ever reaches a point where he ceases, utterly and completely, to be a child. In a business society, money, while not everything, comes first. Money does not come first, however, in the life span of a human being. Any given piece of protoplasm has to spend at least a few years when he cannot put money first, because he is physiologically unable to do so. Unfortunately, the kind of treatment he gets during those years of dependence sometimes turns him into an adult who has, not a greed, but a need for money. I have been a parent long enough to have gotten rather bored with the phrase about the rejected child. But tedious or not, children do get rejected—all up and down the income scale. And when they grow up, how it shows!

Periodically, in the American press, we have campaigns to expose what is called corruption. Athletes, civil servants and other fallible human beings are revealed in the papers to have taken money they should not have taken. And as most Americans are aware, the corruption which is exposed in the papers is only a fraction of the corruption which actually exists. The exposure of corruption by the newspapers is a mug's game, since this kind of behavior is routine in the high, the middle and the low places of American life.

And yet, curiously enough—though Americans have something of a reputation for unashamed candor—one never finds an American who says, "Yes, frankly, I have been corrupted by money." The reason Americans do not say they have been corrupted by money, even when the evidence is unmistakable, is that they do not feel corrupted by money. And they are right. Money does not corrupt people. What corrupts people is lack of affection. What corrupts people is being exploited, either emotionally or financially. What corrupts people is being treated with contempt or indifference. What corrupts people is the business society's intolerance of weak and helpless individuals.

What corrupts people is being brought up mechanically by parents who are obeying the injunction to get ahead. What corrupts people is the unstable family, besieged by a million entrepreneurs to whom the family—except one's own, of course—is a meaningless clump of potential customers. What corrupts people, very often, is being chivvied and pressured into the narrow mold of profit-making behavior when their real desires lie in other directions.

137

People are never corrupted by money, which is why the periodic campaigns to "clean up" corruption never accomplish anything and have to be endlessly repeated. Money does not corrupt people. Money is simply the bandage which wounded people put over their wounds.

Medicine heals wounds. Sometimes Nature heals wounds. Bandages do not. In our money society, we have a phrase which we use all the time without ever thinking of its implications. We say of this or that man that he is "worth" such-and-such an amount of money—fifty thousand dollars or half a million dollars or ten million dollars. But the phrase is a booby trap. To whom is a man worth this or that specific sum of money? To God? To his wife? To the American housewives for whom he produces extremely useful or practically valueless consumer goods? To the next generation? Above all, is a man worth this-or-that sum of money to himself? Does ten thousand dollars or ten million dollars represent—can it ever represent—what a man thinks about himself?

On this subject, Abraham Lincoln once wrote with a good deal of relevance. Some years before he became President, a New York firm applied to him for information about the financial standing of one of his neighbors.

"Yours of the 10th received," he wrote. "First of all, he has a wife and baby; together they ought to be worth $500,000 to any man. Secondly, he has an office in which there is a table worth $1.50 and three chairs worth, say, $1. Last of all, there is in one corner a large rat-hole, which will bear looking into."

The fabulously rich, the most brutalized and degraded poor, and the people in between must all arrive on this earth via the uterine process; and they must all spend a much longer time being weak and helpless than the progeny of other mammals. How much money, then, is enough to take the place of the family? Obviously, no conceivable amount. Money, over and above the needs of protoplasm, will not stabilize and fortify the family one is currently engaged in raising. Neither—and this is the saddest part of all—will it heal the wounds left by a family upbringing which was lacking in compassion and generosity.

This is a bitter truth, but a little bit more is gained by facing up to it than is gained by a life of permanent and fruitless flight. There is no more painful experience in the world—it is possibly just as grim as death itself—than the realization that one has not been loved. If American adults concentrate on the present and the future, and seldom spend much time mulling over and trying to appraise their own pasts, it may be because—for many of them—being a child in an expanding business society was in essence a cruelly lonely experience.

How much money is enough? How much money is enough for bodily needs? The people who live on the subsistence level could answer this question quickly enough. And grimly enough, too. But in trying to figure out how much money protoplasm needs, I do not mean how much it needs to drag out a wretched and greatly impaired existence. Wealthy alcoholics also suffer from malnutrition. In fact, that is what often kills them. Nothing is gained by finding out how little people *can* live on. The question is how much money do people, considered as flesh and blood, *need*? The two things are not the same. The question should perhaps be revised to read: How much money is enough for protoplasm, if the protoplasm is to function with a maximum of satisfaction to the owner?

It is not a question which can be answered simply or quickly. Merely taking pencil and paper and writing down, "So much for food . . . so much for rent. . . ." will not bring us to an answer. There is a complicating factor which has to be allowed for. This complicating factor has recently been exhaustively explored by Dr. David Riesman in a book about Americans whose title I always think of when I go to my supermarket in the Saturday morning rush. The title of Dr. Riesman's book is *The Lonely Crowd.* In it, Dr. Riesman makes a point which has to be kept constantly in mind when trying to calculate how much money is enough for protoplasm. Dr. Riesman points out that—with the dizzying speed of movement which is a feature of societies based on getting ahead—the United States has changed from a "producing" nation to a "consuming" nation.

The United States is still discussed, in the public prints, as if it were a country with an open frontier and a primary concern with producing. It was my little girl, however, who brought it home to me that Dr. Riesman is right— that in the comparatively short time between my childhood and my daughter's, the business society has ceased urging people to produce and is now exerting its very considerable influence to get them to consume. When my daughter grew old enough to walk and talk, I was dismayed to realize that she was perpetually asking me to buy her toys. At first I had that dismal and unnerving thought which periodically visits all the conscientious parents who have read the books—the thought being, "Perhaps the child acts this way because her mother doesn't love her enough."

On further reflection, however, I realized that her chronic plea for toys is by no means peculiar to her. The other children seem to behave in a somewhat similar fashion. I also realized something which has already been mentioned in Chapter I of this book—that when my contemporaries and I were small, it was not possible to make very much money out of children. Now, however—what with Hopalong Cassidy suits, detonating cereals, comic books and an endless succession of incredibly flimsy toys —children are a gold mine to American business. When my mother took my sister and me into a grocery store, there was nothing in it but groceries. But when I take my little girl to buy groceries, she cannot get three feet inside the door before confronting a large rack filled with comic books, storybooks, coloring books and children's victrola records. If she is always asking me to buy her things, it is certainly due in part to the fact that American business is always trying to sell her things.

Like most people my age and older, I have a vivid memory of the United States when it was still a "producing" society. When my sister and I were small, we got presents at Christmas and on our birthdays, and those two occasions stood out from the rest of the year with a wonderful luminosity. When we were small, one doll a year was par for the course. In the present-day consuming society, however, it is literally only a matter of months before the wetting doll is succeeded by the doll that says, "Coo-coo"; and this in turn is succeeded by a doll whose hair can be given a permanent wave; and this is again succeeded by a doll whose hair can be dyed. The next step, obviously, is going to be the doll that can get pregnant.

At the period of American history when I was growing up, thrift was a virtue which was by all means to be instilled into the children. We also had, in our neighborhood, a phrase which has now gone completely out of use. It was a phrase about "teaching children the value of a dollar." The children of my generation were trained—more or less unthinkingly, but nevertheless thoroughly—to be hard-working little producers. Consuming was something which respectable people approached in a cautious and gingerly fashion.

The spender, in earlier days, functioned as an individual. He made a choice of what to buy and what to refrain from buying, and the choice meant something. Currently, however, the spender—even little teeny ones, like my daughter—does not make a choice. He just buys everything. Everything he can pay for, and possibly a few things he cannot. This does not mean that my little girl was born a wastrel. She is responding to pressure—pressure that is superlatively well organized and that never lets up.

My principal objection to the business society's seduction of my daughter is not that the toys are shoddy and overpriced—though this is true. My principal objection is not that the twenty-nine-centses mount up, over the period of a year, into a formidable sum—though this is true, too. My principal objection to the seduction of my daughter by American business is that, being by nature a conservative, I am a firm believer in the joy of ownership and the pleasure of possession; and I should very much like to have my little girl learn to experience those delightful sensations. But as Mr. Charles Lamb pointed out a good many years ago, in his *Essay On Old China,* you cannot get the true heft and savor and exquisiteness of owning, if you own very much.

Thorstein Veblen, writing about American business when it was still in its producing stage, alluded in a famous phrase to the "conspicuous consumption" of the well-to-do. What characterizes American business in its subsequent development, however, is the inconspicuous consumption of my little girl with her reiterated plea for gimcrack toys. When it comes to answering the question, therefore, of how much money is enough for protoplasm, what must be kept in mind is that we have split personalities and therefore live in a state of chronic unease. This chronic unease makes us particularly vulnerable to the unceasing sales pressure of American business. The business half of our society has finished with its producing stage, when people were urged to work hard, spend cautiously and put money in the bank which could be used to conquer the frontier and build up American industry. The frontier is gone, and American industry has been built up to a point which is unparalleled in human history. The business society, therefore, now wants us to be professional consumers—thoughtlessly but wholeheartedly dedicated to buying things, wearing them out, using them up (or possibly just getting bored with them) and then buying more things to replace them. It gets us to do this by promising us happiness, in addition to the merchandise. So we buy.

This kind of behavior is good for business, but bad for protoplasm. Business societies come and go, but protoplasm, like Tennyson's brook, goes on forever. It is protoplasm—and not the advertisements, or even the editorials and think-pieces—which furnishes the only truly reliable yardstick by which we can measure our behavior. Protoplasm needs food, shelter, affection and intervals of relaxation. When it does not get these things, it kicks back. The question of how much money is enough for protoplasm is, obviously, a question which the business society does not want us even to ask, much less try to answer. But while it is true that we are all the creatures of our society —and to a much larger extent than we usually recognize-- it is also true that a society does not necessarily have to be taken lying down.

The answer to a consuming society is to dig one's toes in and resist the pressures. The answer to a consuming society is to make one's purchases—not "instinctively" and in unthinking response to sales stimulus—but slowly, reflectively and in the full awareness of what one is doing.

Protoplasm does not need its hair curled or its fingernails tinted, and it does not need a new dress because everybody has seen the old ones. In a consuming society, all buying is considered good; but the fact of the matter is, that there are several different kinds of buying, and not all of them are good.

The curls, the fingernail polish and the new dress are what might be called defensive buying—designed to avert criticism, to make one pleasantly inconspicuous and to evoke at least a fugitive sense of belonging. Then there is escape buying. Escape buying includes all the things purchased in order to give one a temporary sense of power in a life situation—i.e., the business-dominated United States—where one feels permanently powerless. (Of the permanent sense of powerlessness, more will be said in the next chapter.) Protoplasmic buying is most obviously illustrated by the purchase of food, and here the ability to consume—in comparison to defensive and escape buying—is very sharply limited.

One of my own ways of rebelling against the consuming society was to stop taking the Sunday paper. There was a time—and it was not so very long ago—when I read punctiliously and with devotion all the advertisements which are so conspicuous a feature of our Sabbath journals. I did not read these advertisements because I had any money to spend. It was merely that I felt "hep" and "adjusted" and au courant if I knew what was being offered for sale. But I am a working mother, and I can only maintain that two-headed status by a sort of niggardly attitude about the

145

expenditure of time and energy. I discovered that Sunday seems a much longer day, if one does not take in the Sunday paper. Not only much longer, but much nicer. He knew what He was doing when He rested on the seventh day.

Seasoned parents will want to know what, if I do not approve of my daughter's torrents of toys, I do about it. It must long have been apparent that this book is not being written because the author is happily conscious of being a good mother and eager to share the secret. On the contrary, this writer is full of shattering qualms about the performance of maternal duties, and being the methodical daughter of a methodical father, wants to know the reason why. So far as my little girl's continual request for toys is concerned, I have a quota for her and I try to stick to it.

However, my husband and I are like most parents in that we have wonderful theories about parenthood, but when actually confronted by our screaming or sobbing child, we often give a fairly good imitation of that imperishable Saxon, Ethelred the Unready. I maintain a consistent attitude of disapproval toward non-protoplasmic spending; but my featherweight consumer does not pay much attention to it. If it is actually true, as we are told, that example is better than precept, then she may in the end come around to her folks' point of view—since with frankfurters at $.83 a pound, we are pretty much held down to protoplasmic spending through sheer force of circumstance. As to the quota, I cling to it with a certain amount of tenacity, but the little woman has been known to get the better of me. By unscrupulous methods, of course. Nevertheless, it is something of a comfort to have a definite policy; although a definite policy always gives you a sense of guilt when you do not live up to it.

How much money is enough for protoplasm? The question can only be answered by a long and careful scrutiny of one's buying habits; and by a breaking down of purchases into their basic categories of defensive buying, escape buying and buying for protoplasm. Defensive buying and escape buying are spending which is done in the hope —a hope doomed to disappointment—of stabilizing one's relations with other people. It is not, for example, defensive or escape buying to purchase a ticket to a play. It is both defensive and escape buying to pay $20 for a seat in order to see the play—and be seen at it—on the opening night.

The question of how much money is enough for protoplasm can, of course, be of interest only to people who are living above the subsistence level. In this discussion of money, not much has been said about the people who live on the subsistence level. This is partly because I have myself never lived on it; although I am like most middle-class people in that the mere passing fancy that I might be reduced to such a strait is enough to bring out the sweat on my forehead.

However, save as producers of guilt feelings in luckier human beings, the people on the subsistence level are not influential. If they were, they would not be on the subsistence level. Obviously, the Americans whose thinking about money is going to be the most influential are the

Americans who have got some to think about. But in a consuming society, with its constant sales pressure on chronically tense human beings, it is easy to feel that one is on the subsistence level when one is actually somewhat above it. Emotionally, of course, we are all on the subsistence level. But the answer to that chilly situation does not lie in the steady disbursal of funds.

The idea of using the needs of protoplasm as at least a partial answer to the Eggcup Civilization is not, I am sure, going to pass without challenge. The first and most spontaneous objection is likely to be, "But my protoplasm is rather special. It needs more money than other people's." This argument can safely be shelved until such time as it cuts some ice with an undertaker. A more respectable objection is likely to be, "But my need for beautiful pictures and beautiful fabrics and beautiful rooms is so basic and so chemical that it could certainly be described as a protoplasmic need."

However, the aesthete can justify his existence only by being artistic about the process of living itself. To be artistic about the process of living means that one's life, when it is over, should add up to something. To paint great pictures adds up to something. To buy great pictures—in preference to looking at them in museums—does not. It is impossible to express personality by spending money, even when the money is spent on the most priceless and beautiful objets d'art. To paint a picture one's self, even if it is execrable, is an expression of personality. But purchasing is not, and never can be, a form of self-expression; and the purchase of Beauty Itself is just as much escape buying as spending fifteen cents for a comic book.

Another objection to using the needs of protoplasm as a key to buying is likely to be made on a humbler, but much more important level. By women, it may be argued that the curls, the fingernail polish and the new dress—characterized here as defensive spending—are really protoplasmic spending, since without them, a woman could not either get married or stay married. This, to be sure, is what it says in the advertisements; but is it really true? Is there any way of wearing either a rhinestone pin from Woolworth's or a square-cut emerald so as to suggest that the wearer is tenderhearted, sympathetic, sensible, maternal, sexually undamaged, responsible and intelligent?

The pressure on American women to spend their way into womanliness is so enormous and unremitting and inescapable that it almost takes a decompression chamber to get away from it. Two thousand times a day, literally, the American woman is assured (a) that any woman who is not young and pretty is not a woman at all and (b) that any American woman can be young and pretty if she just buys this-or-that. In view of the pressure involved, it seems a little harsh and demanding to classify the curls, the fingernail polish and the new dress as defensive spending. But not to classify them thus is to go along with the advertisers (and the businessmen who hire them) in saying that a woman—just in and of herself, and without a nickel in her pocketbook—is less than the dust beneath the chariot wheels.

In a business society, women are one of the unbusiness-like minorities; women are a depressed class. Thus the curls, the fingernail polish and the new dress are certainly the most defensible of all defensive spending. But it is well to keep in mind a certain weird but comforting truth. In despite of the movies, the advertisements and popular fiction, women are in a position from which they are unlikely to be dislodged—no matter how little they spend on personal adornment. They happen to be the only other opposite sex there is. And a woman continues to be a woman—since there is, after all, nothing else she *can* be—for several decades after she gets her first wrinkle.

In asking the question of how much money is enough, it must be conceded that Americans are not ideally situated for finding the answer. We have to resist, not only the formal and organized pressure of the advertisers, but also the informal pressure of the people we come in contact with. My husband and I are probably not vastly different from many Americans in that we have both acquaintances and kissing kin who are strongly of the opinion that we do not earn and spend enough money. (The spending is important. Just earning it would not be sufficient.)

This is not to say that these are not nice people. Some of them are extremely nice—witty, intelligent and markedly generous. But they agree with the manufacturing Brahmins that all buying is good. They themselves do a great deal of defensive and escape buying; and they cannot completely hide their belief that if we would just shake off our sloth and get to work—neither of our professions being considered to merit that stern and beautiful word —we could easily acquire enough money to furnish our barren and makeshift second floor. The business society does not have to be taken lying down; but standing up to it requires a conscious effort. It is not child's play.

How much money is enough? I have not answered this question specifically, in terms of dollars and cents—nor do I intend to. For any given American, it is a personal matter, and it has to be worked out by the individual in terms of his own life situation. Furthermore, since the question is an individual and a personal one, it goes without saying that it does not have to be answered on behalf of anybody but one's self. If the reader wants to know what to do about his pleasant, generous, charitable, likable friend who is rich as Croesus, the answer is simple. Nothing. Let him take care of his own dualism. Nobody else can.

For the unquestioning disciple of the business-money-success society, no conceivable amount of money is enough. A parent does ultimately reach the end of the road. The children inevitably and unpreventably grow up, and for better or worse, the job is finally over. But nobody ever gets to the top in the business society, because in the business society, there is no top. Not if the top is defined as a place where one can rest from his labors (as my father could) in the contented knowledge that there is no further to go.

In the upper echelons of the business society, the quest for money is usually transformed into the quest for power

—power to mold public opinion, power to sway one's own or other governments, power to manipulate the lives of millions of strangers. But the Unholy Grail of power is just as frustrating as trying to achieve peace and dignity through more money than protoplasm needs. Power, like charity, begins at home. There can be only one life, the manipulation of which affords any real and lasting sense of triumph. That is one's own.

VII

The Rising Tide of Helplessness

———

THERE IS SOMETHING which needs to be said in a hurry. I have mentioned using protoplasm, and its comparatively simple needs, as a guide to buying. (For people above the subsistence level.) This does not mean, however, that anything is gained by turning off the water at the main and getting the aqua pura in buckets from the nearest stream. This writer's attitude toward protoplasm is one of respect, not unmixed with awe. I believe in treating it generously, no matter to whom it belongs.

Because of the age group into which I was born, I have been able to reminisce about the United States when it was still a producing society. I do not think, however, that either I or any of the other parents would be benefited by a return to the horse-and-buggy days. Mothers of small children do not usually have much wish to go back to the time when frozen foods, vacuum cleaners and washing machines had not yet come into general use. I am not, therefore, looking for a way back. I am looking for a way forward. But the way forward involves a slight exploration of the defensive and escape buying which use up such a large amount of American energy—sometimes to the unintentional detriment of the children. It also involves taking issue with some of the folklore and mythology about business which comes between us and reality.

There are a great many people in the United States who are weary of the kind of behavior which stems from the profit motive. Some of these people are individuals who have themselves showed no inconsiderable talent for earning money or making profits. But we all, business people and anti-business people alike, cling to the profit motive—disillusioning as it has shown itself to be. We cling to it because, according to business folklore, it is inextricably tied up with something we should quite properly be loath to relinquish—advanced medicine and labor-saving devices. The American business society, being the dominant one of our two societies, is in a positon to make its official contentions stick. And it is the official contention of the business society that if we dispense with profit-making attitudes, we automatically revert to the Stone Age—to operations without anesthesia, to early deaths and infant mortality and making soap in a caldron over a wood fire.

The fact that this belief is almost universally held in the United States—even by people who have no particular love for American business—does not necessarily make it valid. In the past forty years, the business society has benevolently lightened the burden of homemaking to an almost unbelievable degree. What it took my mother hours to do, dusting and scrubbing on bended knee, I can do —with my vacuum cleaner and its attachments—in half an hour and standing nobly erect. But I am assured—all American housewives are assured—that we may only have our vacuum cleaners on the condition that souped-up junior executives give themselves ulcers trying to make more profit for their company than is being made by the vacuum cleaner company down the street.

This is taking a very limited view of junior executives. These junior executives go home to their wives and families, at the end of the business day, and try to be as kind and wise and full of vision as their state of fatigue permits. (We may safely assume that the junior executives have children, as the business society is considerably imperiled if they do not.) These junior executives go to P.T.A. meetings. They conscientiously endeavor to spend some time with the children. They have the children's teachers to dinner. If the children are in difficulties, they talk to a child psychologist or go to lectures on parenthood. For the sake of their own and other people's children, they sometimes take an active part in community activities.

The junior executives have, in short, two kinds of behavior: daytime behavior and evening behavior. It is the business society's inflexible contention that their daytime behavior represents the way they really want to behave.

It is the business society's contention that nobody in the vacuum cleaner company—employer or employees—could be induced to produce good vacuum cleaners except under the circumstance of grueling competition for money and financial advancement. But this has never been proved. And, indeed, it is a lower and more unflattering estimate of the American male than your correspondent is disposed to make.

If the junior executives' daytime behavior represents "human nature," their evening behavior represents "human nature," too. So far as anybody knows, it is perfectly possible for human beings to produce good vacuum cleaners without being flogged on from the rear by the wish for financial gain. The placid conviction that it is a fine thing for babies to have clean floors to play on and for mothers to have time to play with them could, quite conceivably, be a sufficient impetus for producing good vacuum cleaners. No one has ever succeeded in establishing any intrinsic connection between advanced medicine and labor-saving devices, on the one hand, and profit-making, on the other. The connection has been made. It has been made in the minds of practically everybody. But it has never been proved—any more than it has ever been proved that the Pueblo Indians' rain dances actually make it rain.

Ten or twelve years ago, when I was a feverishly gay divorcée, I spent more on myself alone than is now spent on my little brood of three. The gradual retreat from comparative luxury which has characterized the last decade of my life was not, as might be imagined, humiliating or degrading. On the contrary, it brought with it a certain feeling of freedom. For this feeling of freedom, I am somewhat indebted to the anthropologists. When I began reading in the social sciences, I took it for granted—as do most Americans—that the United States, with its liberating and humanitarian machines, represents the highest type of civilization yet developed by the race of man. But this apparently cheerful assumption raises, for a good many people, a disturbing question. "If the United States is the finest flowering so far of the human race, then why am I not happier in it?" Despite the advertisements and the Bath of Perfection, human beings know themselves to be incurably imperfect. Hence they are often driven to answer the question despairingly. "Well, there must be something wrong with me."

The anthropologists do not back themselves into any such dismal corner. To them, the United States is simply one of many societies, past and present, which resemble each other in having both advantages and disadvantages for the people who live in them. This point of view is rather a jolt at first; but upon getting accustomed to it, it is remarkably emancipating. The social scientists do not say that the United States is the best civilization yet developed. Instead, they ask, "Best for whom? For the children, perhaps?" We have the report of Margaret Mead that Samoan society, for instance, is much easier on children and young people than the American business society.

I am an amateurish and undisciplined dabbler in the

157

social sciences, but they have nevertheless had a considerable effect on the way I run my house and spend the family funds. Reading about people in non-business societies—or even in business societies other than ours—made some of my previous rituals in pursuit of having things nice seem rather unnecessary and, indeed, a bit tribal and primitive. I save a good deal of time and energy by reason of the fact that to me, the Duchess of Windsor is just another aborigine—though no doubt a very pleasant woman.

This does not mean that I know how to live serenely in a money society. I do not. As has already been noted, nobody—literally nobody—rises above the society which bred and trained him. One of the sources of tension between me and my little girl is the fact that she does not know how to hurry; whereas I am so much the creature of my time and place, that I can seldom make myself stop hurrying. In theory, I believe in leisure; but I can only act slowly and deliberately when my teeth are clenched. Nor have I been able to achieve, with my best efforts, any more than a partial and tentative freedom from that atmospheric training about money which all Americans receive.

I worry about money, as my publishers can testify. I rebel against it by not keeping my checkbook balanced. I am inclined to be sour and uncharitable about people whose old age seems in a fair way to be nicely cushioned. And when it comes to being the captive of materialism and empty show, it must be admitted that this volume would have been published a month sooner, had I not been tempted beyond my strength to paint the kitchen.

In making the statement that in a divided society, there are no pure types, I know whereof I speak. However, by no longer having the money to spend which I once had, I more or less accidentally achieved a little free time in which to speculate upon the nature of spending.

A good deal of what Americans buy, beyond the needs of their human flesh, is bought either as a defense against or an escape from an environment which is intuitively felt to be harsh and unfriendly. As described by one who has done a great deal of it, defensive spending is spending which is done to avoid being considered odd and peculiar and in order to have something to talk about with other people. Most of the purchases of television sets come under the head of defensive spending. So does a good deal of the money laid out in the United States for clothing and cosmetics. Defensive spending is peculiar to the United States, and is not nearly so characteristic of the Western European business societies as it is of ours.

In order to understand the necessity for defensive spending—and it actually is necessary—a few comparisons must be made with the other business societies. If the people in the Western European business societies do not go in as much for defensive spending as we do, it is not simply because they do not have the money, and we do. The answer lies further back in time than that. Among the other business societies, the United States is unique. It is the most highly developed of all the business societies. It is the one in which business activity is the most far-flung, all-pervasive, intensive and extensive.

The United States is also the business society in which, at the present time, radicals, crackpots, left-wingers, intellectuals, Utopians, eccentrics and various other sound and unsound critics of the social order get the roughest and most intolerant treatment. The Western European business societies are in considerably more danger of Russian invasion than we are, but they have not been characterized by the hysteria, smear tactics, witch hunting and merciless punishment of nonconformists which have blotted our escutcheon. England, France, Holland and Belgium have not even produced—much less elevated to a position of prestige—any such quirksome and erratic moralists as Elizabeth Bentley and Whittaker Chambers. When it comes to eccentrics, deviants, saints and sinners, the other business societies ride the punches.

This is not to say that the English business society, to take one example, is made up of nobler people than ours is. The English fell just as hard as we did for the illusion that money, over and above the needs of protoplasm, makes people happier and that making money therefore comes first. H. G. Wells and D. H. Lawrence were among many English writers who discoursed with biting eloquence about the disastrous effect of British business on British life and character. And when it comes to grinding in the faces of the poor, the early British industrialists of the nineteenth century hung up something pretty close to the world's record. The gin-sodden misery of the British working classes, in the opening years of the Industrial Revolution, has not been paralleled in the United States.

The English business society, however, has evolved more slowly than the American business society. The reason for this comparative slowness of pace lies in the fact that England, like the other business societies of Western Europe, is a small, long-settled country with a great many years of English history behind it. Much of the prosperity of these other business societies—while they were prosperous —was based on the fact that they had colonial empires. The point worthy of especial note is that these colonial empires lay overseas. The populations thereof did not have to be absorbed by the folks at home. The United States, on the other hand, was in a manner of speaking its own colonial empire. Unlike the other business societies, when the United States expanded, it had to absorb, too. Or try to.

The English, like the other Western European nationals, have lived together for a long time. They know each other well. The English do not speak of Scandinavian-Englishmen, Spanish-Englishmen or Irish-Englishmen as we speak of Scandinavian-Americans, Spanish-Americans or Irish-Americans. The Americans have not lived together for a long time and they do not know each other well. The United States, compared to the other business societies, is a nation of strangers in a bulky and variegated homeland. The United States is still on its shakedown cruise.

It was probably inevitable that in the United States, the Eggcup Civilization should reach a peak of development unequaled in the other money societies. American business is not generally regarded by scholars and classicists as a thing of beauty and a joy forever, but it has nevertheless performed an amazing job. It has done something which the businessmen in the other business societies did not have to do. It has welded together into a social unit a huge and heterogeneous population with no uniform history behind it and not even a uniform climate in common. The welding job was accomplished by inducing everybody—from the Atlantic to the Pacific and from the Great Lakes to the Gulf of Mexico—to buy the same things at the same time.

But although the job was amazing, it was fruitless. American buying cannot do for the Americans what English history has done for the English. By making people ashamed and afraid to wear old clothes and drive old cars, it is possible to give them a certain superficial resemblance to one another. But it is not possible to give them much comfort in their hearts, or the kind of unity that will stand up under pressures like the Battle of Britain and twelve years of scanty, rationed food. American business and American buying have not been able to give the American something he needs very badly.

That something is the sense of belonging—the sense of being a part of something larger, older and better established than any single individual could be. The other business societies are smaller, poorer and less efficient than ours; but history and geography have conspired to make them more homogeneous. Between one Frenchman and another, there are two thousand years of France. The people in the other business societies, therefore, do not have to look for brotherhood through buying things to the same extent that we do. What is significant about American purchasing is not its volume—although that is the only thing we ever hear about it. What is significant about American purchasing is the unconscious search for unity and kinship which lies behind a good deal of it.

It is important to recognize defensive spending for what it is—money down a rathole. Defensive spending is money laid out for a momentary respite from a harsh and narrowly critical environment—i.e., the business-dominated United States. Defensive spending is money laid out for protective coloration. It is money spent both to keep from being talked about and to have something to talk about. But its effects, though temporarily benevolent and relaxing, are not permanent. It does not permanently alter for the better the impossible relationship between the warmth-seeking human being and the most highly developed business society in the world.

Another form of American spending, escape buying, is also money down a rathole. Escape buying has already been mentioned as having its roots in the feeling of personal powerlessness. All human beings want and need intervals of feeling personally powerful. They want and need power over their heavenly garment of protoplasm so that it will digest peacefully, sleep restfully, respond sexually and in general perform to the gratification of the tenant. They also want and need power over their environment—power to make the environment produce food and shelter, power to make their votes felt in the government, power to make their opinions felt with the local School Board, power to develop their talents in whatever direction those talents want to go. But for all his society's magnificent conquests of Nature, the one thing the mid-century American has not got is the feeling of personal power.

One reason for this aching void is that, economically, we actually are powerless. Only the merest handful of mid-century Americans, compared to the total population, is in a position to throw its weight around economically.* This is not anybody's fault. What happens when a business society moves is that, in a manner of speaking, the money drifts to the top and the people drift to the bottom. *All* the people drift to the bottom—the ones who appear to be riding herd, as well as the ones who appear to be ridden.

The congregation of producers and employers grows continually smaller (and lonelier and more frightened) and the congregation of consumers and employees grows continually larger (and lonelier and more frightened). The phrase "labor and capital" goes out of use and is supplanted by the phrase "labor and management." But "management" is simply a collection of employees whose salaries will buy them anything in the world except a chance to take the bit in their teeth. With the natural evolution of American business, we are becoming a nation of hired hands. And not, unfortunately, the kind of hired hands who sit down at the table with the family.

The drift of a business society is toward impersonality.

---

* To be sure, the American can make himself felt as part of a pressure group, but this is not *personal* power.

In human terms, this means everyone suffers, in his role as a person. As has already been noted, American chronic unhappiness is no respecter of incomes. Because of the underdevelopment of affection and the overemphasis on aggression, competitiveness and skepticism, personalness—like privacy—is going out of our society. When that happens, the personal human being—no matter where he stands on the income scale—suffers increasingly from the feeling of having no personal power. Only by purchasing—whether it be a pair of kitchen curtains, a baronial estate, an extra pair of play shoes, or somebody else's long-established business—can he have a momentary sensation of having some avoirdupois to heave about. The point to be emphasized is that the sensation is momentary. It does not last. The buying has to be done over and over and over again.

Another element which is responsible for the feeling of personal powerlessness lies in a simple but drastically important fact. Although the United States is dominated by its business society, most of the people in the United States are not businesslike. The children are not businesslike. The women are not businesslike. The people who educate the children are not businesslike. The people who work for the government are not businesslike. The artists are not businesslike, and neither are the aged, the ill or the unemployed. Even the businessmen themselves are not businesslike after five o'clock. At least, they hope they are not, and they try not to be.

If the question is put—What is escape buying an escape *from?*—the answer is that it is an escape from a situation which, to Americans, is well-nigh intolerable. That situation can be summed up as follows: That with the automatic and unplanned evolution of the business society, American business is coming increasingly to dominate the unbusinesslike American population in a fashion which is painfully similar—in operation if not in intent —to the way the Communist Party dominates the Russian population.

The merest nodding acquaintance with Russian history, however, indicates that the Russians have been accustomed for a great many centuries to having no personal power. They are not brought up to expect it. Americans, on the other hand, have had—up to now—the liveliest expectation of feeling personally powerful. When, in some apparently mysterious way, that feeling does not materialize, they feel baffled, frustrated and cheated, and they take the only way out which seems to be open. Either with resplendent cash or on the installment plan, they buy things over and above the needs of protoplasm—seeking, even though it is only for the moment, the enhancing and entrancing sensation of being dominant, of being responsible and of having things under control.

It is the feeling of having no personal power which lies at the bottom of many of the quarrels Americans have with each other. When a person is haunted by the feeling of having no personal power, he always assumes that although he does not have it, somebody else does. The banker thinks that the union leader must have it. The union leader thinks that the Chairman of the Board must have it. Actually, of course, nobody has it. The drift of money to the top and people to the bottom, characteristic of an uncontrolled and swiftly evolving business society, cannot be laid at the door of single human beings. It is simply the natural, unsurprising and inevitable result of applauding profit-making characteristics and of rejecting the Bankruptcy Qualities as weak and unmanly.

Two things are primarily associated with the name of the United States. Money and machines. Both American machinery and American corporate finance are so awesomely intricate that no single human being can hope to master either of them, in their entirety. But Americans have the reputation of being the fellows who know what makes things tick. The fact that they cannot construct or operate a calculating machine which can remember a million separate items, or that they do not know what you do when you want to sell the Empire State Building, gives them—once again—a horrifying feeling that the environment is out of control.

Americans accept the obligation to know how things work, and when they cannot meet the obligation, they feel depressed and helpless. But perhaps the environment is not out of control. Perhaps it merely seems out of control because our approach to it is wrong. The important question about American machinery and American finance is not, "How do they work?" The important question is, "What is their purpose?" If one understands their purpose, it is not necessary to know how they work

167

To the question, "What is their purpose?" the answer is not complex, but exceedingly simple. The purpose of American machinery and American corporate finance is to make money. And the purpose of the money is to compensate for the underdevelopment of affection. The purpose of the money is to provide the security and stability which can only properly be supplied by the family, past or present. The purpose of the money is to provide a defense in depth against the rigors and uncertainties of existence which, in actuality, can only be supplied by the Bankruptcy Qualities. The purpose of the money, on all economic levels except the subsistence one, is to serve as a sort of emotional Scotch tape for holding together people who, through no fault of their own, might come unstuck without it.

This purpose is, of course, foredoomed to failure. But although the picture seems a cheerless one, it should be recollected that the business society is not our only society. If there is an answer to the question of how much money is enough—and there is—that answer comes to us, not from the business society, but from the anti-business America. If there are better methods of defense and escape than relying on money for magical results—and there are—those methods must be looked for in the anti-business society. If there is a place in American life where one may expect to find simplicity, instead of numbing complexity, that place is in our official national morality—the Judeo-Christian ethic. It would now seem to be time, therefore, to give a little study and attention to the other side of the coin.

VIII

The Successful Failures

___

Wʜᴇɴ I was a child, the householders in our neighborhood used to lean on their rakes, on Saturday after-
noons, and "talk politics" across the privet or barberry
hedges. Politics, however, was not the province of women
and children, and what the political complexion of our
community was, I could not say. I do recall that my father
was president of the local Civic Association for several
years when it was at its most active and efficient. And my
mother—though astronomically shy and completely allergic
to the platform and the dais—accepted, out of a sense of
duty, the presidency of the P.T.A. for one year.

No particular emphasis was placed on these activities,
and I recall, in addition, that my mother did not join the
Red Cross during World War I. The Red Cross women
rolled bandages in the basement of the public school every

Wednesday night, and I remember hearing my parents say that the good ladies were inefficient bandage-rollers, were too gossipy and were more concerned with the becomingness of the white coifs they wore than with the staunching of blood. In our household, not much allowance was made for human weakness—the unstated philosophy being that the Deity had put us on this planet for the express purpose of overcoming it.

What my parents stressed verbally, in bringing me up, was "proper" behavior and "being a little lady." What they actually handed down to me was the idea of participating in some way in community life, and the further idea that one could afford to be a little thoughtful about this participation. I should like to pass on to my daughter at least as much as was handed down to me, and I think it would be convenient for her if I could do it a little less blindly. Children need love, as everyone is prepared to admit. But they need something more than that—and this is a point which is too often overlooked in the books on child care. They need a clear definition of what constitutes personal virtue.

All human beings have a deep craving to be "moral" or "good." "Goodness," of course, means different things in different parts of the world and at different periods of history, but the important question for the compassionate American parent is what it means here and now in the United States. To trace the outlines of the American business society is easy enough. It is the dominant one of our two societies; it is literally never silent; and it invades in some way or other every single one of our waking hours. But to define and understand the anti-business society is a much harder job.

It will readily be understood that this chapter is going to be more difficult for both reader and writer than the preceding ones. It involves what is known to the trade as a change of pace. Any cheerful and self-confident house-wrecker can point to where people are doing the wrong thing. The results tell the story; and destructive criticism is downhill work. But to discover (a) what is the right thing to do and (b) how to go about doing it is slow, pain-ful, tedious, unpopular and generally uninviting. It has nothing to recommend it except that the children need to have it done.

Furthermore, "goodness" and doing the right thing al-ways involve intangibles. The business society has given all of us One Hundred and Ten Easy Lessons in putting the tangibles first—the house, the car, the furniture, the clothes, the television set, the Rembrandt original or the week end at the Waldorf. Even with the best will in the world, it is hard to shake off the semi-hypnotic influence of American business. And it is the view of American busi-ness that the tangibles come first, and the intangibles exist only to be snatched up at the last minute—just in case there should, after all, be a God and we should be lucky enough for Him to be a half-wit.

Here is perhaps as good a place as any to make an ex-planation. A great deal is being said in this book about the Judeo-Christian ethic. The present writer is not, however, trying to prove anything about whether that ethic is, or is not, of divine origin. The whole point about it is that it was meant to be used. It may have come down from Heaven, or it may have been worked out by a pastoral and by-no-means-wholly-Caucasian society at the eastern end of the Mediterranean. Its function, however, not its origin, is the important thing about it. And its function is to give meaning and purpose to life. Its function is to guide people's behavior so that they will do the minimum of harm either to themselves or to other people.

By this time it is perhaps also unnecessary to add that morality does not mean only sexual morality. A good many Americans have been alienated from the Judeo-Christian ethic by the circumstance that, in the hands of our forebears, it often seemed to stand for rigid sexual repression and for very little else. But punitive sexual codes are a misuse—not a use—of ethics, which are designed to embrace all human activities and not just one.

Hence, although the admission is probably disastrous, not much attention is being paid to sex in these pages. In a business society, the role of sex can be summed up in five pitiful little words. There is money in it. In a business society, where everything else, from diapers to death, is commercialized, sex is obviously going to be commercialized, too. Although a great deal of anxious attention is paid to American sexual problems, they seem to this writer to be a symptom—a surface phenomenon—and not a first cause. In a society where tenderness is a Bankruptcy Quality and the province of nincompoops, sex is obviously going to be baffling and unsatisfactory to a great many people.

I am one of those not-very-highly-regarded little house-wives who is bathed in sex all day long by American advertisers. They disguise it by calling it "glamour." I am inclined to think, however, that the process of making tidy profits by pandering to the poor old housewife's dreams of glamour sometimes ends up with the biter bit. At least, I deduce from reading the newspapers and the novels on the best-seller list that the satraps and pro-con-suls of the business society are as much victimized by cast-iron notions of Perfect Love, Perfect Romance, Per-fect Beauty and Perfect Mates as are we hewers of wood and drawers of water. One gets the impression that the exploiters differ from the exploited only in having a little more mobility. The advertisers and the public-relations gentlemen are sometimes free to wear themselves out run-ning after the dream, whereas the housewife does not usu-ally get much chance to drag her anchor.

It does not occur to us often enough that this sub-stitution of glamour for sex—and other equally dubious substitutions—is the work of the communications indus-try. This writer is aware that in discussing the American communications industry, she is practically begging to have her ears pinned back. There is a belief in the United States—as firmly clung to as a canon of sacred law—that only newspapermen, ex-newspapermen, publishers and cinema tycoons can speak with intelligence and authority about the communications industry. But I am endeavoring to hack out a little clearing, in the wilderness of money and myths, for my daughter to grow up in. Speaking simply as a parent, I cannot afford to recognize anybody —however illustrious or well-seasoned—as an authority on the communications industry whose experience of that industry does not include frequent pressure from a tiny consumer to buy Howdy-Doody Cookies.

Hacking out the clearing means trying to identify and recognize the other of our two American societies—the anti-business America. In this search, there are two preliminary jobs to be done; and the first of these is to assign the American communications industry—the movies, the popular magazines, the comics, the newspapers and radio-television—to its proper place in the scheme of things.

One of the major tenets of this book is that American life, in reality, is not nearly so complex as most people think it is. And the relationship of the American population to the communications industry is extremely simple. We are dependent on it. The dependence is not a healthy one; but as I will not do my daughter much good by chasing rainbows, it may as well be frankly admitted that very little can be done about this dependence—except to recognize and understand it.

We are not dependent on the output of the communications industry because that output is prevailingly wise, creative, challenging, inspiring and spiritually nourishing. It is admitted by all thoughtful persons that this output—at least, as far as advertising and entertainment are concerned—is for the most part shabby and tawdry. Compared, at any rate, with what it could be. We are nevertheless dependent on that output because, being Americans, we are tortured by conflicting goals and we therefore cannot afford to spend much time alone with our thoughts. Those thoughts, followed to their logical conclusions, would be too dismaying. The enormous influence and great prosperity of the communications industry, consequently, are not due solely to the virtue and intelligence of the communicators. They are based in part on the uncertainty, tension and fatigue of the communicants.

My little girl's father is in the field of adult education, and that means evening classes. When I am working alone around the kitchen, after my daughter has gone to bed, I usually turn on the radio. Since I am totally unmusical, symphonies are not my cup of tea; and for us tone-deaf clods, the evening radio fare is depressing and mechanical to a degree. I am, however, an American and a product of the American environment; and my tolerance for silence is therefore not very high. Forced to choose between an inferior distraction or no distraction at all, I choose the inferior distraction.

As has already been mentioned, in our household we do not take in the Sunday paper. Every seventh day, the United States—no matter what desperate straits it is in— has to get along without any attention from my husband and me. To date, the neglected commonwealth has always managed to squeak through anyway. But the first few Lord's Days this regime was in operation, my helpmeet

175

had to ask—like Odysseus going past the sirens—to be tied to the mast.

Tense people—trying to live decently in the cynical, competitive and unaffectionate business climate—need distraction, even if it is only the unsatisfying distraction of reading what other tense people have to say about Korea, Indo-China or the Russians. Similarly, the fact that a great many Americans turn the knob and light up the dial does not actually *prove* that they do it with a pleasant feeling of anticipation. A great many prisoners pick oakum, but not usually after they are sprung.

To say that the bond between communicators and communicants is not a uniformly noble one is not, however, to condemn the communicators out of hand. The American communications industry is the most visible (and audible) of all American businesses. It is the mouthpiece of all the others, who, without it, would have no way of reaching the consumer except through contagious enthusiasm about the merit of their products. The communications industry is not only the most conspicuous of all American businesses, but it is also the one in which the division between the two American societies is most painfully apparent. It is an outward projection—an externalization, as the psychologists would say—of that uncomfortable and exhausting indecisiveness which, to a greater or lesser degree, afflicts all American-trained human beings.

Of all American businesses, the communications industry is the one most in need—from the point of view of the human beings involved—of compassionate appraisal. The steel industry does not have much trouble keeping the wolf from the door, and it is not without influence on American life. But most Americans are not vividly conscious of the girders and I-beams which hold up their stores, office buildings or apartments. The communications industry, on the other hand, makes a great deal—though not all—of its money out of banality, clichés, hackneyed old stereotypes and safely uninspired points of view. The banality and clichés are not decently hidden behind cement blocks or brick facing. They are right out there in the open for the customers to feel—consciously or unconsciously—dejected and frustrated about. Or angry and openly critical.

Nor is it only the customers. The communications industry suffers from a hideous and terrifying disability. It has to hire sensitive, well-educated people. Within its seething bosom, communications probably contains more disappointed, disillusioned and unhappy individuals than any other outfit in the bright hierarchy of the market place. Young Americans go into heavy steel with no further notion than that they will make money by participating in the production and distribution of that commodity. Toward communications, however, young people are frequently drawn by the idea that they will have a chance to set down an honest and fruitful reaction or two to life as they find it. (And perhaps also make money.) Expecting to be primarily communicators, and only secondarily businessmen, they discover that, in any business, it has to be the other way around.

177

But once having tasted the heady wine of communicating—even watered-down, as it is in a money-and-success Republic—it is virtually impossible to change course and resign one's self to selling steel. Unlike the people on the other side of the fence, communicators are born, not made. In our country, however, they are not born under a lucky star. The ghosts of Shakespeare and Tacitus do not pay much attention to heavy steel, but those mocking and derisive shades are always picking bouquets of nettles for the crossed-up people in the word business.

The American communications industry produces three things—advertising, entertainment and information. To the charge that its advertising is frequently vulgar and its entertainment more often than not pitiable, the industry does not customarily react with very much heat and spirit. But in its role as a news-gathering agency—in its function as a collector and distributor of "the news" or "the facts" or "the truth"—it is a red-hot champion of itself. And, indeed, even among the communicants, a good many honest and intelligent people believe that communications does penance for its sins and justifies its existence by its role in distributing the news. Where the news is concerned, even fairly sophisticated Americans generally take it for granted that the press and its sister institutions operate—at least in a rough sort of way—as a vessel of truth.

As has already been noted, however, we recognize truth by the fact that insofar as we can lay hold of it, it sets us free. It is liberating. It clears away superstitions and crippling misapprehensions. It dissolves tension. We recognize truth-seekers through the fortunate circumstance that in five thousand years of recorded history, the human race has produced quite a few of them. Euclid and Sigmund Freud were in pursuit of truth, and both of them succeeded in capturing a segment of it. Between Euclid and Sigmund Freud on the one hand, however, and the American news-gatherers on the other, there is an important distinction. Euclid and Sigmund Freud were not also in business.

The news-gatherers cannot give us all the facts. There are too many of them. The news has to be edited—there is no way around that. And since the news-gatherers are in business, and bound by business convention to make the maximum possible amount of profit, what they give us is not "the facts," but the *salable* facts. A fact, of course, can be true in the Euclidean sense and still be salable. On the other hand, the circumstance of its being true in the Euclidean sense sometimes makes it completely unsalable— at least, in the view of a success-minded management which believes that even the news must entertain and which is in a position to operate on this somewhat peculiar theory.

The claim of the press and radio-television that—where the news is concerned—they serve at least approximately as a vessel of truth can by no means be entirely disallowed. On the other hand, it cannot be accepted without a certain amount of scrutiny. The matter boils down to a fairly simple question: How much emancipating truth can you collect, put together and distribute when your first and primary obligation—or even your secondary obligation—is to show a profit and keep the banks and the stockholders happy?

The answer is not long and wearisome. Some, but not enough. Some, but not enough to quiet the troubled conscience. Some, but not enough to satisfy the creative instinct and leave the creative person feeling contented and fulfilled. Some, but not enough to be wholeheartedly accepted as an authority and a leader of men. Some, but not enough to keep the communicants from going off by themselves every four years and electing their own boy to the Presidency.

In our time, the news-gatherers—and especially well-known columnists, political reporters and foreign correspondents—are regarded with respect, attention and reverence because they are supposed to have the "inside dope." But this suggests a query. Why should there *be* any "inside dope"? If a man writes a column or a newspaper story, and tells all the facts, then the reader of that piece is just as well informed as the writer. The dope—that is to say—is outside. If the man writes the piece and does not tell all the facts—if the dope remains inside—then the reader is entitled to ask why some of the facts were withheld.

Was the writer afraid of losing his job? And if so, what may be inferred about the purity and integrity of his employers? Or did the writer think it would not be good for the reader to know all the facts? And in that case, where did he—or his employers—derive the authority to act as an arbiter of what is good for the reader?

Access to the wire services does not heal the painful split in the American personality. It merely gives the people who have it a great deal of information. It does not teach them how to use the information. It is not a North Star by which they can navigate. The American communicators probably suffer more from the rift in American life than any other group of employers and employees in the country. It must be said to their credit that, in spite of the difficulty, they appear to handle the split personality about as well as anybody else. *But they do not handle it any better.* If there *is* any "inside dope"—that is it.

In examining the claim of the news-gatherers that they serve as a truth-disseminating agency, a distinction must be made between truth and information. It is often said of Americans—indeed, we often say it of ourselves—that we are a pragmatic and practical race of people and that we like "the facts." A fact, however, has no life of its own. It is mere deadwood until it is put together with other facts to make a structure which has usefulness, significance and purpose. It is not quite accurate to say that Americans like "the facts." There is a certain kind of fact which we like—the isolated fact. The enormous success of "Information, Please" and similar sorts of quiz shows is evidence that we like the truth—but only when it is an orphan.

Karl Marx once said that religion is the opiate of the people. In our country, however, it is not religion but information which is the opiate of the people. One New York radio station concludes all its news broadcasts with the announcement that an informed America is a free

America. Actually, America is in the process of being smothered by information—of a certain type. Along some lines, America is not only informed. It is overinformed.

If a well-known movie star travels in Europe with a man not her husband, no expense is spared to make the folks at home aware of the situation. But having gotten the information, what are we supposed to do with it? Write the girl a letter and tell her to come home? This is only one, all-too-easily duplicated example of how communications—trying desperately to live up to its two self-imposed obligations of purveying the truth and fattening up the exchequer—gets off the Euclidean beam. Information we have in abundance, but a good deal of it is pointless, useless and extremely difficult to be practical or pragmatic about. And some of it—as the Lindbergh kidnaping so dreadfully illustrated—we are just simply not entitled to. "Human interest" slides by the easiest of gradations (and degradations) into subhuman interest.

In the last analysis, what counts, in communications, is content—not noise or volume or infinite repetition. It is often said that the late President Roosevelt owed a great deal of his popularity to radio. One may regard Franklin Delano Roosevelt's impact on the American social structure as good or bad, but the social structure would have felt that impact, even if radio had not been invented until after Mr. Roosevelt died. Radio simply hastened a process that would have taken place anyway.

President Roosevelt had something to say to his grateful electorate—or beggarly adherents, however one chooses to describe them—which, at the time, they wanted to hear. Had radio (or the newspapers) not been in existence, people would have written each other letters about it or passed it on by word of mouth. It was the content of the Fireside Chats, not the fact that they were on the radio, which accounted for their great influence. Had the content been unacceptable, not all the money or "promotion" in the world could have forced the American public to listen to them. The business society conditions and influences us because we cannot get away from it. The Chief Executive, however, we can get away from.

Radio cannot take the credit for having "made" President Roosevelt without also taking the blame for having "made" Hitler. Actually, of course, machines are unselective and do not discriminate between one sort of user and another. What counts, in communication, is content; and what also counts—although not enough attention is paid to the fact—is the communicants. The communicators, defending themselves against the charge that so much of their output is utterly ordinary, sometimes say that the masses of the American people have the mind of a twelve-year-old child. The indictment is not as damning as it is intended to be. An affectionately treated twelve-year-old child has more on the ball than a warped, despairing cynic of forty-two. And history has already demonstrated that there is a highly significant difference—in terms of mass behavior—between the twelve-year-old American communicants and the twelve-year-old Germans.

If one is trying to trace the outlines of the anti-business

183

America, the communications industry is the last place in the world to look. The reason for this is simply that these outlines are not what is called newsworthy. The anti-business America is based on Christian morality, and the goal of Christian morality is for people to get along well together *outside the framework of making money*.

Some of our giant corporations go in rather heavily, in their personnel programs, for what they refer to as "human relations." In fact, "human relations" is the new twist in modern management. Wistful management yearns to get off the cross of gold. But since management's "human relations" must always be conducted within the suffocating confines of profit-making, they are jinxed from the start.

To the extent that non-money-making human relations are successful—as Negro-white relations were successful at the Stage Door Canteen, for instance—they are not messy, bloody, lurid, dramatic, provocative or exciting. They are not, in the communicators' view, salable. It is possible, of course, that the communicators may be making a mistake about the salability. Some pre-industrial observers came up with just the opposite opinion. "How beautiful upon the mountains," they said, "are the feet of him who bringeth glad tidings, who publisheth peace."

The American communications industry is a business. Save for the one particular of being more shot through with personal anguish, it differs in no respect from any other American business. Therefore it cannot speak for the anti-business America. In its output, occasional transient inklings and fugitive glimmerings of the Judeo-Christian ethic can be discerned. But not the mother lode.

The business society makes the secondary mistake of treating both its enemies—Communism and the Judeo-Christian ethic—as one and the same thing. But it does not make the primary mistake of failing to recognize an enemy when it sees one. When the American ethic goes into action—when, that is, American human beings put it into action—those Americans are almost invariably treated by communications as the enemies of business. And therefore of itself. In this, the communications industry is quite right. Such Americans actually are the enemies of business. Business has a great many enemies. It also has a great many captives, not all of them willing.

The place to look for the Bankruptcy Qualities is, so to speak, among the bankrupts. Parents cannot hope to accomplish their job—much less enjoy it—unless they are able to pass on to their children some fairly workable idea of what constitutes personal virtue. In this responsibility, the movies, the popular magazines, the comics, the newspapers and radio-television are not of much use to American fathers and mothers. Those flourishing institutions have little to offer parents except the somewhat quavering assertion that they have found out how to serve both God and Mammon. On the subject of personal virtue, the source and the authority is the anti-business America.

If the anti-business America is to be grasped and made to yield up some of its riches, the communications industry must first be seen for what it truly is. And there is yet another job which has to be done. This second job is to retrieve the phrase "do-gooder" from the ignominy which currently surrounds it. If further proof is needed that communications speaks for the business, and not for the anti-business, society, one has only to consider that the American press is responsible for the fact that the phrase "do-gooder" has a highly uncomplimentary connotation to Americans.

This connotation, the communications industry has succeeded in selling to everybody. Probably the only point upon which American liberals and American conservatives are in complete agreement is the belief that the phrase "do-gooder" should be surrounded by quotation marks, when written, and inflected condescendingly, when spoken. My little girl, if she is alive fifty years from now, will not be able to hear the inflections. But the quotation marks will still be on the record. And I think she and her contemporaries may find it extremely puzzling that "doing good" should have been regarded, by mid-century Americans of every conceivable type, as a bad thing.

In the United States, in the middle of the twentieth century, the best the do-gooders * can expect is to be apologized for. "He's a do-gooder, but he's a swell guy anyway." Only do-gooders of exceptional personal charm rate this accolade. True, it seems like a rather grudging plaudit; but compared to the way do-gooders are usually men-

---

* From here on, I shall omit the quotation marks. They are too much trouble.

tioned, it is positively doting. That a do-gooder is an un-attractive person is, in our day and age, taken for granted. But perhaps it should be explained, for the benefit of fu-ture generations, that not everyone is agreed as to why do-gooders are unattractive.

Sometimes they are considered unattractive because it is assumed that they are simply disguised cynics. It is as-sumed, that is, that they have cooked up some ingenious little racket which pays off very well and have chosen to conceal it behind a sickening display of virtue. Of course, the people who take this view of do-gooders are more un-consciously self-revealing than they would consciously choose to be. A second reason why do-gooders are consid-ered unattractive is that they are believed to be meddling, interfering busybodies. "Meddling," however, is a mean-ingless word unless one also states what the meddler is meddling with. A surgeon who removes a tumor could be described, in the strictest accuracy, as meddling and inter-fering with the course of Nature. And as a matter of fact, there have been times in the history of medicine when certain physicians were referred to, with considerable heat, in just this way. My little girl, too—if she were old enough to use the words—could certainly point to occasions when she considered my behavior both meddlesome and revolt-ingly intrusive.

For the benefit, once again, of a future generation, it should be explained that nobody is antagonistic toward do-gooders because they have high ideals. In the United States, everybody has high ideals. What makes the do-gooders unattractive is that they act upon these ideals and more often than not, the action is rather fumbling. If there is one thing the American people cannot stand, it is a fumbler. The American, steeped to the eyebrows in precision machines, feels more relaxed and at home with a competent, skillful evil-doer than with a good man who is all thumbs.

Another reason why do-gooders are considered unattractive is that they are always on the defensive. This permanent defensiveness is usually explained as neuroticism. But while it is quite true that do-gooders are always on the defensive, this behavior is not neurotic, but completely rational. The do-gooders are always on the defensive because they are always in danger of attack. To do good in a money-and-success society—even fumblingly, even amateurishly, even part time—is to thumb one's nose at the tribal totem pole of personal advancement and financial prowess.

The last, and possibly the most telling, argument against the do-gooders is that they are so often overearnest and humorless. Against this charge, they cannot be defended— except possibly by suggesting that it is not so much that they are overearnest and humorless as that they are over-earnest and humorless about the wrong things. In their long and active careers, neither Governor Dewey nor Senator Taft has ever been taxed with being a muddleheaded do-gooder; but their very own lieutenants are reported in the public prints as sighing a little sadly over the fact that Presidential timber is sometimes just that.

In trying to grasp, define and put to better use the other America—the anti-business society—it is of the utmost importance to salvage the phrase "do-gooder" and relieve it of its present connotation of knavery and idiocy. The words "do-gooder" mean exactly what they say. A do-gooder is someone who does good. A do-gooder is someone who either preserves or improves life. The most illuminating way to define a do-gooder is to describe him in terms of his opposite. The opposite of a do-gooder is not, as might be supposed, a do-badder. The confirmed do-badders are almost all confined in institutions. In the normal walks of life, the opposite of a do-gooder is a talk-gooder.

A society split the way ours is split produces, understandably enough, a bumper crop of talk-gooders. A talk-gooder, however, is interested in virtue; whereas a do-gooder is interested in his own personal virtue. The difference between the two is roughly commensurate with the difference between being dead or being alive. The talk-gooder applauds generously (and breathes a sigh of relief) when some person or persons two thousand miles away gets a Caucasian church opened to Negro communicants. The do-gooder says shakily, "Bring me my bow of luke-warm gold," and tackles his own "hardheaded," "realistic" vestrymen.

Do-gooders, in the United States, are in such undeservedly ill repute that very little has been said or written about them—in the communications industry, at any rate —except in the way of uneasy condescension or contemptuous dismissal.* There are, nevertheless, enough of them so that they can be divided into two kinds. Usually, the phrase is employed in a socio-political sense; but the words have a basic, philosophical meaning which needs to be understood before they are whittled down to the narrower political meaning. To use "do-gooder" in this basic, philosophical sense—meaning someone who preserves or improves life—is to see immediately that there are millions and millions of do-gooders in the United States. Mothers, for instance. Or housewives. Or schoolteachers. Or civil servants. Or musicians. Or research scientists. To mention only a few examples from a list which could be considerably extended.

This is only another way of saying what has already been said: That although the business society dominates the United States, most of the people in the United States are not businesslike. The business society, with its communications industry, is the dominant one; but the anti-business society has the broader base. And despite the unpleasant aroma which is attached to the word, if there were not millions and millions of do-gooders in the United States, we should, long before this, have been at one with Nineveh and Tyre. The crucial point, however—and the one which is of most interest to parents—is that most of these do-gooders are not drawing down the dividends of prestige and self-respect to which their behavior entitles them.

---

* One minor exception must be noted. Do-gooders are sometimes very kindly spoken of when they are far, far away. Father Damien and Dr. Schweitzer get a wonderful press.

They are being cheated. They are being cheated because American business, while it does not frown on helping the human race, frowns on people who start right in helping the human race without first proving that they can sell things to it.

The philosophical do-gooders—as, for the sake of convenience, they might be called—are not usually conscious of being do-gooders. They preserve and improve life, but not always in the full awareness of what they are doing. They are conscious, though—at least, in a dim sort of way —of being regarded by American business as pretty poor sticks. Of course, in their role of consumers, they receive a great deal of attention. As long as some part of the weekly pay check remains in their pockets, the business society courts them like an enterprising call girl. But as fully rounded individuals, as people who have a job to do and who do it—the job of preserving or improving life—they are either ignored or actually abused on the grounds that they are slothful and do not "work."

In the business society, to "work" means to make money, and it follows as the night the day, that the less money made, the less "work" involved. As Margaret Mead has already pointed out, in *Male and Female,* a woman who earns $50 a week as a stenographer is spoken of as "working"; but when the same woman brings up three children on the $75 a week earned by her husband, she is spoken of as "doing nothing." Similarly, a woman who works in a factory or office, as well as taking care of her family, is referred to as a "working" mother. The phrase suggests that

191

there is such a thing as a nonworking mother. But among the matrons who take care of their own offspring, no such thing exists.

On the so-called audience-participation shows, a woman who does not earn money always refers to herself as, "Just a housewife." Upon questioning, it usually turns out that this woman has somehow managed to steer a family through depressions, inflations and wars with no further resource than the wages of a pharmacist or a garage mechanic or a mailman. She nevertheless takes over, without question, the business society's idea of "work." She would have to be a genius, not to. Schoolteachers, of course, are painfully familiar with the American fiction that teachers, while admittedly not well paid, are recompensed by having an infinity of leisure.

Among my own souvenirs, I have a priceless sample of the fiction that people who do not have a great deal of money to show for it do not "work." During the war, while my husband was overseas, I wanted to dull the rigors of separation by fatigue. I wanted to find a job that would get me thoroughly tired out; and I discovered one that met the specifications perfectly. In the winter of 1944-45, I worked as a teacher's assistant with the six-year-olds in a small school in Brooklyn. One rainy day, when the children had not been able to get out to play, I went for dinner in the evening to the home of a businessman who, though unqualifiedly successful, is perhaps a little less subtle and knowledgeable than most. By the assembled guests it was observed that I looked pale and tired. My host turned to me in genuine astonishment. "But how could you be tired?" he said. "You get out at three o'clock, and besides, it's only children."

The broad base of the anti-business society is formed by the philosophical or unconscious do-gooders. By the business society, these unwitting Samaritans are regarded, not as do-gooders, but as no-gooders. They are parasites. They do not "work." But if one is to see life steadily and see it whole, it is not always safe to assume that the voice of business is the voice of God. The standard defense of the business society—back in the good old days, when people outside the Kremlin were allowed to criticize it—used to be that the businessman is born businesslike and that his pursuit of money is "human nature." In the last seventy or eighty years, however, we have learned—we have learned it as parents, if not in any other way—that "human nature" is whatever human beings feel like making it, and that "human nature" varies considerably from place to place and era to era. In fact, it is the responsibility for shaping "human nature" which weighs so heavily on the conscientious mothers and fathers.

In the mid-century United States, we seem to have two kinds of "human nature." The pressure of business-minded people on young and malleable American males has produced what is recognized the world over as a type —the successful American businessman. In the bright lexicon of business, this type has its opposite number. Opposite, and inferior. The opposite of the successful American businessman is The Type That Fails To Make Money. All the huge minorities in the business society—women, children, Negroes, artists, schoolteachers, sick people, bookkeepers, stenographers, and so on—are lumped together under the convenient but misleading label of The Type That Fails To Make Money.

Once a human being * has been identified as belonging in this category, he has been taped as an undesirable and you have said all that needs to be said about him. There is an ideal American type—the money-maker—and he either could not or would not live up to it. He is a drag on the wheels of progress, and it sometimes requires a portion of the taxpayer's luscious, hard-earned money to keep him alive. Or well. Or working (no quotes) at some job which does not produce much money. Money means "results." One of the sad effects of this equation is that the schools of the country are chronically behind the eight ball, since they do not, and cannot, produce "results."

The successful American businessman has been trained to exercise one narrow and particular talent, and he exercises it. He has been trained to make money, and at the same time to make dutiful noises about "serving the public," and he does just that. To say that a human being is a successful American businessman is to describe him

---

* Or a group of human beings, like a tenants' association, or a share-croppers' league, or a defensive alliance of consumers, or the dingy brotherhood of the Okies and the "wetbacks," or clumps of pigheaded professors who will not sign loyalty oaths.

fairly accurately—at least for eight of the sixteen hours he is (presumably) awake. In the United States, there is only one way of making money, and that is by being aggressive, competitive and skeptical.

There are, however, dozens of ways of failing to make money. It is one thing to fail to make money because your single talent happens to be a flair amounting to genius for translating the plays of Aristophanes. It is quite another thing to fail to make money because you are a Negro. Or a child. Or a woman. Or because you want to run a small farm. Or because you want to be a nurse. Or because you have religious convictions against making money. Or because you went to West Point. Or because you do not enjoy the society of people who think too much about making and spending money. To say that a human being has failed to make money in the United States of America, is to say nothing about him at all. The description covers sexual degenerates, Abraham Lincoln and everything in between.

In refusing to accept as a reality the ignominy which attaches to The Type That Fails To Make Money—in asserting the crucial importance of the philosophical or unconscious do-gooders who preserve or improve life—I should not like to be taxed with a sentimental overevaluation of the American people. I am not disposed to grow saccharine about "the little man" or "the common man" without first asking what is meant by "little" or "common." But the single fact of having failed to make an impressive amount of money does not, in itself, prove anything. It does not establish incompetence. Neither does it establish virtue. I therefore go no further along the road of sentimentality than the unarguable fact that human life is still going on in the United States.

Very few people die in our streets. Rioting, though not unknown to us, is sporadic. Somehow or other American children do learn to read and write. The position of the Negro has improved, and if, as Mr. Gunnar Myrdal says, this is 70 per cent due to the efforts of the Negroes themselves, it only goes to show that "doing good" is not limited to the Caucasian race. If human life is still going on in the United States, it can only be because a goodly part of the population is more interested in—and better at—the job of preserving and improving life than in the job of making money. If human life is still going on in the United States, it is not because we have a business society. It is because, fortunately, we also have an anti-business society.

Children belong to the anti-business society; and so do all the people who think that taking care of children is a serious and important job. (Some of these people, especially if they are males, also belong to the business society —which is only further evidence that a split society means a split in the single human being who has got to live in it.) The anti-business society has no communications industry. It operates for the most part by personal contact, force of example and word of mouth. But—with the distinguished exception of Lord Chesterfield—personal contact, force of example and word of mouth is the way parents operate with their children. (Or where they fail with their children, when they do fail.)

The most important question of our time and place is, "What constitutes a good human being?" Nobody tries harder to answer this question than some of the business-men themselves. But they do not succeed in answering the question because they do not ask it at the right time in their own lives. They ask it when they are fifteen or six-teen—which, practically speaking, is too early. Then they do not ask it again until they are forty-five or fifty—which is too late. Among the more articulate businessmen—the ones who participate in forums, symposiums, and seminars and who write thoughtful pieces for the magazines—the good human being is defined, by implication, as the proven success in business who then turns to "serving the commu-nity."

This is what might be called, not so much the "noblesse oblige" as the "richesse oblige" theory of the good hu-man being. Of its several weaknesses, there is one so completely fatal that no others need be discussed. It leaves mothers out of the picture. Were women to accept whole-heartedly the "richesse oblige" theory of the good human being, the business society would commit suicide quite neatly but effectively by simply not producing enough children to keep going.

During the 1930's, it was fashionable to glorify the un-derdog. Today, merely to speak of him kindly is consid-ered proof positive that the mentioner is a card-carrying member of the Communist Party. Neither of these attitudes is particularly sensible. The underdog exists; but his subordinate position does not, in and of itself, ennoble him. Nor does the position of the upperdog prove anything in particular about his superiority, although he is certainly America's Dream Boy.

It is a fact beyond challenge that both the underdog and the upperdog finally end up in the grave. And well before they reach that terminal point, they are both under the urgent necessity of asking, and of answering, the question of what constitutes a good human being. If a good human being is a person who preserves or improves life, then, clearly, there are millions of good human beings in the United States. But we are prevented from seeing the clear, true outlines of the anti-business society by reason of the fact that the business society and the communications industry have tacked a lethal rider on to the notion of the good human being.

The business society does not object to people who preserve or improve life. It merely says that they cannot be considered good human beings unless they have also got the ability to attract money out of other people's pockets and into their own. Some few of the philosophical or unconscious do-gooders who keep human life going in the United States do happen to have, in addition, the talent for making money—usually by some unique skill or creative gift. But compared to the total number, they are an infinitesimal minority. And when the concept of the good human being is so narrowly limited that only a very few

198

special people can lay claim to it, the society which supports that concept is in trouble.

The trouble is not, however, hopeless or incurable. We do not suffer from a shortage of good human beings. But the fact must be faced—bizarre as it may seem—that the great majority of them are, and always will be, unbusinesslike and basically indifferent to business. The anti-business society exists. It operates. Its broad base is the philosophical or unconscious do-gooders. And while the business society is the dominant one of our two societies, the anti-business society is the indispensable one.

This chapter can be no more decisively concluded than by quoting from the section on Religion in a book by two British sociologists entitled *English Life and Leisure*:

"But even among people who are indifferent to the Church, and find that it has no answers to their problems, there is not infrequently a spiritual hunger, a wish that there was something in which to believe. It was put well in one of our case histories by an elderly man of the lower middle-class who said,

" 'Is there nothing for me to believe? It's no good going to church where people read out prayers they don't really believe themselves. But there must be something. There is so much love and unselfishness in the world among all the evil things. And just look at those (pointing to a row of sweet peas in full bloom). You can't tell me that's all just accident. After all, people know the difference between right and wrong, and what's beautiful and what's ugly. I'm old now, and I'm not afraid to die, but I wish I could understand more clearly what this "good" is that we can feel and see. It would be a help to people to get it organized a bit. . . .' "

It is now time to turn to the human beings who do organize it a bit—the socio-political do-gooders.

IX

How to Be Happy,
though American

———

I F THE DISTINCTION between the talk-gooder and the do-
gooder seems to this writer an important one, it is
partly because I have been both myself. When I went to
college, I picked up what were referred to as "liberal"
views; and when I was in my twenties, I defended these
views with heat and spirit in whatever drawing room or
front parlor I found myself—one of these front parlors
being my father's. I did not, however, do anything about
my opinions, except verbally. Once in a great while the notion would go through me like a dagger that after all, talk
is pretty cheap; but like Scarlett O'Hara, I said I would
think about it tomorrow. Personal problems preoccupied
me—getting married, being married, going to Europe,

writing a book and trying to figure out how to behave after the book made money.

Nor did I go to the Stage Door Canteen because I knew that, unlike most of its sister institutions, it did not bar Negroes. I went to work at the Stage Door Canteen only because everyone was doing some kind of war work and I was too squeamish to be a Nurse's Aide. But once there, I found myself in the company of a group of people who were going to considerable trouble to put, and to keep, their liberal views in action. I stumbled into the situation by accident, but it seemed like a golden (if slightly un-merited) opportunity to quiet the conscience which I had picked up during my American childhood.

I am not looking backward at the past through rose-colored spectacles. The do-gooders at the Stage Door Can-teen were fallible human beings. They had, by the end of the war, thousands of letters from Negro servicemen—and a few from white servicemen—as testimony that the racial equality they believed in and practiced had not been a failure. But the administration of that policy involved the usual clashes of temperament. There was the usual inter-necine warfare. There was the usual nubbin of really ma-ture individuals; the usual nubbin of unreliable self-dramatizers; and the usual collection of indispensable, half-and-half people in between. It was nevertheless a group with a firm foundation in the American ethic; and belonging to it taught me something which was to come in handy later on, when I had a child to bring up.

There are fashions in children, just as there are fashions

in necklines and hats. The child who is currently at the height of the mode is the child who can get along well with the group. The parents who suffer the most anxiety —sometimes, I think, unnecessarily—are the parents whose child elects to stay on the sidelines. Because it is considered so extremely desirable to have a child who gets along with the group, a great many American children are sent to nursery school at the age of two-and-a-half or three. To be sure, the nursery school is a necessity for "working" mothers and for families who live in cramped quarters. But it has a position of its own, quite apart from necessity, and that position is based on the fact that it is the first of the organizations which teaches the child the all-important knack of adjusting to the group.

I am disposed to be a little skeptical of this enthusiasm for the group just because it is a group. The group with which I worked at the Stage Door Canteen had a goal which could be respected and it achieved that goal, in spite of various difficulties in the way. But none of the people in it had been intensively trained—as children nowadays are intensively trained—to get along with the group. There are, after all, a great many crucial areas of life where group training is completely irrelevant. In death and birth and bereavement—in eating, illness and elimination—and in that celebrated protoplasmic activity where three is a crowd—it is not of the slightest consequence to be able to get along with the group.

And as far as the group itself is concerned, a chain cannot be any stronger than its weakest link. The important thing about a group is not to be able to get along with it, but to have something, however modest, to contribute to it. My daughter's parents are not actually opposed to her getting along with the group, but we do think she ought to have learned, by the time she has grown up, to ask some sensible questions about any given group—such as, What kind of group is it? What is it doing? What holds it together? What is the caliber of the single human beings who make it up? If a group is only a collection of frightened people, desperately holding hands in an anguish of confusion—a description which fits a good many American groups, formal and informal—that group is certainly entitled to mercy and compassion, but one scarcely need go to a great deal of trouble to get along with it.

The emphasis on having a child who can get along with the group is only one aspect of the larger question of what constitutes a good human being. Who may lay claim to that title? To mention the good human being is to reach, by the most natural of transitions, the subject of the socio-political do-gooder. The socio-political do-gooders are the people for whom the phrase "do-gooder" was originally— and derisively—coined. They are the conscious do-gooders, and they are hereinafter referred to with capital letters to distinguish them from the philosophical or unconscious do-gooders.

The Do-Gooders are the people who welded the trade-union movement out of the misery and degradation of early British industrialism. They are the people who got the vote for women. They are the people who "interfered" with the right of the manufacturer to employ small children for twelve hours a day. They are the people who "meddle" with the segregators of Negroes. They are the "fuzzy-minded idealists" who try, both at home and abroad, to get the nourishing egg into the empty stomach —while the "realistic" business society keeps its eye firmly glued to the price tag on the eggcup.

A customary way of brushing off the Do-Gooders and of getting their worthlessness firmly established is to charge them with never having met a payroll. In a divided society, however, there are bound to be some Do-Gooders who can, and do, meet payrolls. Not many, but some. From the business point of view, the dangerous and infuriating thing about the Do-Gooders is not that they have never met a payroll. The dangerous and infuriating thing about them is that they regard payroll-meeting as a necessity, but not an ideal.

The Do-Gooders are not exempt from the split personality which is the common disease of us all. Each of our two societies is bound to have *some* effect on the thinking, feeling and behavior of any given American. The number of possible combinations is, of course, as high as the number of Americans. But the Do-Gooders have grasped the fact that an ethic is not an ethic unless and until it goes into action. True, they sometimes accept the business society's definition of "work," and suffer hideous qualms because they have failed to make money. And they sometimes —owing to clouded vision or failing strength—make compromises with business behavior which, ideally, they ought not to make. Similarly—on the other side of the street—the ardent disciple of business sometimes gives generously to "good causes," in the secret, wistful and impossible hope that he can somehow get back to the ethic of his childhood and at the same time manage not to anger and frighten his colleagues in the business world. The dualism in American life—it must be constantly borne in mind—is a dualism in the character of the single American.

There is no pure type of the Do-Gooder, any more than there is a pure type of the American businessman. But the Do-Gooders have been sufficiently active to have incurred the official enmity of the dominant society—an enmity which is unhesitatingly expressed by the newspapers, radio-television, the movies and the popular magazines. They have been sufficiently effective to have been publicly labeled—"branded" is perhaps the better word—as people who do good. The interesting question is, Where do they come from? In a country candidly geared to money and self-advancement, what accounts for the behavior of the Do-Gooders? What makes them spend the precious years of the human life span swimming against the stream?

The explanation is easy. In each generation of young Americans, a certain number of emergent men and women stubbornly resist the dominant side of the society and base their lives, as far as they can, on the American ethic. In the popular phrase, they've bought it. These are the people who speak for—and, more importantly, act for—the vast unbusinesslike minorities. These are the people who fight for civil rights. These are the people who organize share-croppers. These are the people who moved heaven and earth trying to save Sacco and Vanzetti from the chair. These are the people who close up tax loopholes. These are the people who resisted the hysteria about West Coast Japanese-Americans after Pearl Harbor. These are the people who try to block the ruthless exploitation of natural resources. These are the people who labor unceasingly to the end that American jurisprudence should not descend to the notion that to be unbusinesslike is to be subhuman. The list could be extended—although not indefinitely.

This chapter, like the preceding one, is bound to be hard going. The difficulty stems from the fact that it is impossible to solve any of the problems of American parenthood unless one is willing to examine some extremely unfamiliar ideas. The idea that a Do-Gooder is not necessarily a ridiculous and embarrassing nuisance (and probably pro-Communist) is as distressingly novel, in American life, as it would be to see the sun rise over what our British cousins rather poetically call the western approaches. But an idea can be dismayingly unfamiliar and still be entirely correct—a point established, beyond any possible, probable shadow of doubt, by Christopher Columbus.

Besides, an idea can always be relied upon to grow familiar, if one stays with it long enough. That is why Do-Gooders are often very highly spoken of after they are dead. The most conservative apostles of American business now take it for granted that we should have public schools for American children and pure food and drug laws to protect American health. But when the American Do-Gooders first launched these proposals, the business society affirmed violently that they would bring us to the brink of ruin. They were the "creeping socialism" of their day.

One of the distinguishing characteristics of the Do-Gooders is that they are intuitive sociologists. They respond to their society as a society, and not as a free-for-all and a rat race. That is to say, they treat the United States as a still-unfinished social organization which needs to struggle toward a more positive unity. The Do-Gooders may not all of them be able to put this reaction into so many words—although for the most part they are an articulate class of people—but their general behavior, and the results they get, tell the story.

A second distinguishing characteristic of the Do-Gooders is that they commit themselves. They cut off their own retreat. They take a stand. Openly and in their own names, they embrace the idea—so offensive to the business society—that people are responsible for other people's welfare. They take risks. They are publicly identified with movements, groups, ideas, professions, organizations or institutions which put people ahead of property. That these groups, ideas, etc., are likely to be unpopular, goes without saying. The way to identify a Do-Gooder quickly—supposing one should wish to do so—is to look behind him and see whether his bridges are burned.

"Doing good" is therefore (it is perhaps hardly necessary to add) not to be confused with charity. To take responsibility for other people's welfare—in the Do-Gooder's sense —does not suggest the kind of responsibility assumed by women who give dances to raise money for a favorite settlement house. This is by no means to impugn the good intentions of such women, but only to explain that the Do-Gooders work in a much larger frame of reference than Christmas trees for tenement children or contributions to the Hundred Neediest Cases.

The Do-Gooders work on the basic assumption that the United States cannot function rewardingly and satisfyingly unless, *as a society,* it takes a measure of responsibility for the dignity of all the people in it. The Do-Gooders, therefore, do not write checks for fifty or a hundred underprivileged children. They take a personal responsibility for putting a crimp in the tribal folklore which leads to rural and urban slums. Charity, seen from this viewpoint, is not an acceptance of responsibility, but an evasion of it. Charitable acts do spring from good intentions. But the point needs to be particularly emphasized that charity does not mean change, and the Judeo-Christian ethic does.

On this score, it will readily be seen that what is called "benevolent paternalism" is not the answer to the split in our society. Notably paternalistic organizations like the Hershey Company and Johnson & Johnson are sometimes pointed to, by businessmen, as examples of business and ethics dwelling side by side in happy unity. But while it is certainly true that benevolent corporations are better than

209

exploitative corporations, the striking fact about benevolent paternalism in the United States is that there is so little of it. And this is hardly surprising. Urgent, imperious pressure is put on young American males to establish their manhood and their grasp of "reality" by getting in there and taking care of Number One. With this kind of training, it is scarcely likely that many of them will emerge, in middle age, with an incurably fatherly attitude toward the people who work for them.

However, the most telling argument against benevolent paternalism is the fact that fatherhood is supposed to be self-terminating. The child grows up. The father dies. A permanent father-child relationship—which is the core of benevolent paternalism—is, as every enlightened parent knows, a horror by all means to be avoided. The baby changes into an adult. The adult changes into a dead person. Societies change. The more determinedly a society struggles not to change—to maintain what is called the status quo—the more likely it is to come popping out in a series of social hernias.

My daughter is not being reared with an idea of "adjusting" her to the business society. By the time she is twenty-five or thirty years old, the business society as we know it today may no longer exist. Change is the law of life. That being so, the way to deal with change is first to acknowledge its inevitability and then to control or direct it in terms of a clear idea of what constitutes a good human being and a good society for human beings. It takes a bit of discipline to acknowledge the inevitability of change; for while human beings like and enjoy growing up (when they are given the chance to), they do not generally like to die. But, on the other hand, to control and direct changes which are courageously acknowledged to be un-preventable is to lay hold of the one thing the mid-century American yearns for and has not got—the sense of personal power.

If American business were truly "realistic," it would acknowledge with becoming candor that it does not take care of its own. American business puts the American busi-nessman in a position where he is more or less forced to be a talk-gooder. And when a person knows enough about goodness to talk about it, he is bound to be unhappy, dis-contented and disillusioned when he is constrained by fear of condign punishment to limit himself to mere talk. When the American businessman reaches what Dante calls the middle of the journey of his life, he has to make a choice. He has to choose whether he will spend the bal-ance of his time on earth being viciously cynical, quietly heartbroken or just plain numb. A society which does that kind of thing to its favorite sons is approaching the end of the road. If American business were truly "realistic," it would acknowledge the imminence of its departure—in the form in which we know it today—and would set about making that departure a neat, orderly and nicely modu-lated demise. The business society underwent some rather radical transformations, under the influence of Franklin D. Roosevelt, and it has by no means suffered its last sea change.

In the meantime, however, there are children to be taken care of. For parents (and others) who are charged with the upbringing of children, the key society, the indispensable society, the society with survival value is the anti-business America—the invisible Republic of the conscious and unconscious do-gooders. This Republic is kept going by unpopular people. It is kept going by "crusaders," "reformers," clubwomen, schoolteachers, labor organizers, social workers, ministers, nonconformists, a very few Congressmen and Senators and by energetic moralists and practicing idealists in other walks of life—up to, and of recent years including, the Presidency. The position of the Do-Gooders in American life is richly ironic; for while the business community fears and despises them, that business community is nevertheless dependent for its very existence on the tempering idealism they put into circulation. No society which officially encourages ruthless self-seeking could expect to perpetuate itself for a single generation if there were not some opposing pattern of human gentleness and human hope.

The anti-business America is silent, but it is by no means ineffective. The Do-Gooders have only the loosest kind of organization—when, indeed, they have any at all. They have nevertheless exerted a traceable influence on the social structure of the United States, and that we no longer have a nineteenth-century, laissez-faire economy is owing to the fact that the Do-Gooders were able to prevent the business society from developing itself right out of existence. In the hotly resented "government interference" with business—which not all businessmen resent—the interference always results in the businessman's making less rather than more money. (When the interference takes the form of subsidies or high tariffs, it is not described as interference.) "Government interference" with business represents the influence of the Do-Gooders, acting to limit the full and free development of profit-making qualities, and to assert the value and worth of The Type That Fails To Make Money.

The basic philosophy of the Do-Gooders is the belief in man's humanity to man (not to mention women and children). This philosophy has found outward expression in such projects as F.E.P.C., social security, unemployment insurance, TVA, minimum wage laws, child labor amendments, school lunch programs, federal aid to education, low-cost housing, the Federal theater, socialized medicine and the "welfare state"—to mention some of the favorite targets of the business society's ill will. To a great many Americans, of course, the above are loaded phrases. To a great many Americans—carefully coached by the communications industry—the above-mentioned institutions suggest nothing nobler than undeserved benefits showered on lazy, self-indulgent people who have no talent for anything but parasitism. The dominant society construes the Do-Gooders' philosophy to mean that hard-earned money should be taken away from successful businessmen and dazzlingly solvent corporations and bestowed on human trash.

But there is an implied comparison here which needs

to be more fully expressed. American business, like all societies, sets up an ideal type for its citizens to model themselves upon. This ideal type is the person who can make money, preferably against odds. The beneficiaries of the Do-Gooder projects are—it must be admitted—too old, too young, too sick, too artistic or too maternal to measure up to this ideal. But how good is the ideal? Is the ideal money-maker also the ideal husband and parent—relaxed, contented and self-confident in those relationships with wife and children where all the money in the world will not make up for inexperience? And if not, how long can the woman-and-child-rejecting business society look forward to renewing itself?

The job of the Do-Gooders as a social force in American life can be summed up in a single sentence. It has been their function to pressure American business into spending money on people the business society does not consider valuable. That the Do-Gooders are now, and always have been, confronted with a huge task, is obvious. But some of our contemporary institutions exist as evidence that they have not been wholly unsuccessful. Moreover, where the Do-Gooders have actually succeeded in wresting concessions from that iron-jawed goddess, Business-with-a-capital-B, the triumph is all the more to their credit in that it has been consistently uphill work.

The Do-Gooders have no organization and no communications industry. The general body of the citizenry has been carefully trained to fear and despise them, and that training is growing more intensive with every passing week. Also, while it is true that the Do-Gooders have certain sanctions—at least, until such time as the Judeo-Christian ethic is heaved bodily out of the window—those sanctions are shadowy and spiritual. They are nothing like as generally agreed upon as the businessman's sanction to take advantage of tax loopholes, to bribe government employees or to take questionable short cuts with the law of the land. The Do-Gooders are nevertheless, so far as our two societies are concerned, on the winning side—the only side, that is, which can win.

I can scarcely claim to be a socio-political Do-Gooder, but if my daughter were looking for a pigeonhole in which to put me, she could perhaps say that I was a socio-do-gooder. At least, I have occasionally been referred to as a "reformer," a "crusader" and a "do-gooder"—and these nouns did not arrive, surrounded by hearts and flowers, on St. Valentine's Day. So far as my own experience of "doing good" is concerned, I can sum it up fairly succinctly. I hated every minute of it (pretty nearly); and if I had it all to do over again, I would do exactly the same thing.

My mother was brought up in the very heart and core of the Victorian convention about female genteelness—which makes it unsurprising that this writer should have been imbued, in the formative years of childhood, with a considerable fear of being conspicuous. But although my upbringing gave me a certain amount of social timidity, I do not have one of the virtues which often goes with timidity. I am not temperamentally patient. The long and often wearisome committee meetings which are

215

an unavoidable part of co-operative endeavor, and the un-
brilliant slowness of progress which characterizes any attempt to put our national morality into action were, to me,
more than a little taxing.

But quite aside from my own personal disqualifications,
the role of the Do-Gooder is not what actors call a fat part.
It is haunted by that most gruesome of all specters—the
fear that one is making a fool of one's self. Besides, the
audience sits on its hands. Americans have a great distaste
for what they call "controversial" issues. This distaste is
natural enough. The American has a built-in controversy
raging within his skeletal boundaries. He does not want
the Do-Gooders hanging about, serving as painful remind-
ers and reactivating the internal conflict he hoped to be
able to forget. The Do-Gooders are sometimes accorded,
by other individuals, a sort of nervous respect; but that is
not quite as comforting and reassuring as being warmly
liked and genuinely welcomed.

Furthermore, the frequent failure of the American family—combined with our national pattern of underdeveloped affection—has produced, here and there in the United
States, some very ugly customers. It is possible to accomplish a substantial amount in the way of "doing good"
without crossing the path of an ugly customer. But the
ugly customers are always there, lurking in the background
and generating tension. The job of the Do-Gooder is always at least faintly overshadowed with the threat of violence, either physical, economic or spiritual; and for some

216

Do-Gooders—Negro Do-Gooders, for instance—the threat of violence is considerably more pronounced than faint.

When I was writing a book about the people at the Stage Door Canteen who launched and carried off a successful experiment in race relations, I used to stand at the window—standing at the window is the way writers get most of their work done—and wonder morbidly whether the book would get a bad press ("crusader," "reformer," "meddler," "fuzzy-minded idealist") or whether it would get no press at all and just sink like a plummet into an ocean of silence. I had had a little first-hand experience of American skittishness about "good causes," and while I knew it was humanly possible to persuade my fellow countrymen of the practicality of righteousness, I also knew that the job was not unlike maneuvering a high-strung horse past a clotheslineful of flapping laundry.

It turned out that I was unduly pessimistic, although this is not a failing to which I am usually prone. I received as much mail on the race relations book as I did on my first and more "famous" one, and the letters were much more gratifyingly thoughtful and provocative. About my first book, a great many people wrote to me because the book was, at the moment, fashionable. About my third book, people wrote to me because they had read it. It is a basic principle of mine to answer all the letters I receive about my publications, since in this era of mass communications, I am committed to the theory of personal contact as the only way to get very much enjoyment out

217

of life. But the race relations letters could not be answered with a mere flap of the wrist. They required care and study, and sometimes even a little research.

At this point, my editor—a woman from whom practical problems slink away, diminished and with their tails between their legs—pointed out that all the letters asked, in essence, the same question. They all asked, "What can I do about race relations right here and now, in this place in which I happen to be living?" My editor then rounded up some money from the gentlemen who work at my publishing house, and some young women who could type from the distaff side of that corporate enterprise, and between the collection of us, we published a monthly Race Relations Bulletin. This bulletin was exclusively concerned with specific and practical measures for according the necessary ration of prestige to Americans of color. In a modest way, the Race Relations Bulletin was not unsuccessful. It was in demand by schools and various religious organizations, as well as by individuals.

We did not ask people to pay for the Bulletin. We sent it to them free. And after a while, the project developed to a point where it needed to be put on a professional basis. We needed to ask people to pay for it, and to get a paid worker to keep it going. At this juncture, I made a rather odd decision. I decided to give it up. The decision was not as freakish and perverse as it sounds. I believe in improving race relations; but I also believe that people cut down their potential value if they do not live a balanced life. My husband had by that time come home from the wars, and we wanted to have a family. In taking care of this family, I did not want to be pressed for time, drained of energy or absent-minded. That was not, however, the fundamental reason for saying good-by to something that all of us who worked on it were rather proud of. The fundamental reason was that I had at length concluded that the greatest service which could be performed for race relations would be to explore the whole national pattern of the inability to love, of which discrimination against Negroes is only one conspicuous part. I had, that is to say, come upon what seemed to me like the key to what is generally called "the minority problem." That key consisted in giving a little much-needed attention to what American business regards as the Mongol hordes of the unbusinesslike.

When I was working on the Race Relations Committee at the Stage Door Canteen, and subsequently when I was writing and lecturing on race relations, my heart was rather accustomed to spend a good deal of time in my mouth. Part of this apprehension was neurotic—I use the word, even though I distrust it—but part of it was firmly grounded in reality. There is no way to be of genuine service to one set of people without making another set of people regard one as their least favorite character in fact or fiction.

Peculiarly enough, the job which I remember as being the most distasteful was a minor one and, as it turned out, empty of results. After *Color Blind* came out, I was invited to join a great many organizations concerned, either directly or indirectly, with improving the status of Negro Americans. But save for a nominal yearly membership in the N.A.A.C.P. and the Urban League, I joined only one. For this choosiness, there was a reason.

If the Do-Gooders and the Do-Gooder organizations in the United States have a fault, it is that they sometimes make the mistake of trying to spread themselves too thin. The temptation is understandable. For my own part, it always gives me an extremely uncomfortable feeling of nervousness and guilt when I decline to contribute to or work for some organization which is doing a job that needs to be done and of which I heartily approve. But the First Law of "doing good" is to recognize one's limitations as an individual and not to bite off more than one can chew.

Similarly, and with the same drift toward overexpansion, the Do-Gooder organizations sometimes unconsciously take over the business society's belief in gigantic markets. They sometimes unwittingly fall in with the idea that if a thing is not "nation-wide," it is useless and futile. "Good causes," however—or rather, the attitude toward human beings on which they are based—cannot be sold like aluminum saucepans. The Judeo-Christian ethic is kept going, in the United States, in the same way it has been kept going for two thousand years. It is kept going by personal contact, force of example and word of mouth. Hence, making a vivid and lasting impression on a few people is much more important than collecting a dollar apiece from half a million people. The day may come when the business society is administered so as to give us advanced medicine and labor-saving devices in terms of Christian morality. In that case, of course, the business society will be totally unrecognizable to those of us who know it today. But Christian morality will never be operated in terms of business customs, because it is concerned, not merely with virtue, but with *personal* virtue.

The solitary Do-Gooder organization upon whose Board of Directors I said I would serve is called The National Scholarship Service and Fund for Negro Students. It was founded by a young woman perceptive enough to notice that there are $11,000,000 worth of scholarships to white colleges in the United States and that most of these scholarships are open to Negroes. However, Negro high-school students—whose families rarely have the money to send them to college—either do not know about the scholarships or else assume that they would not be welcome at white colleges. But a great many colleges in the North and West would be glad to welcome Negro students, if only they knew how to secure any. Briefly stated, it is the purpose of this organization to act as the middleman between the Negro high-school students and the scholarship-offering white colleges which would welcome them. Its introduction of Negro students into well-known preparatory schools has proved to be the most salable fact about it, but it also adds money to the frequently inadequate scholarships, and it is currently engaged in a program of breaking down old barriers in the Southern states by placing numbers of white students in colleges which have hitherto been predominantly Negro, and vice versa. Slowly but surely, it is mak-

ing a dent in an educational setup which only fairly recently was usually considered hopeless.

I was impressed by this line of endeavor because it was
very sensibly and economically utilizing two items which
happened to be in ample supply—Negro high-school students and scholarship-offering white colleges. As money is
conceived of by the big heart and cancer and polio funds,
this organization does not need much. But it does need
some. Part of its funds comes from the Campus Chests of
interested colleges, but the rest has to be secured from
foundations. The only possible use a Board Member can
be is to help in meeting the modest budget. So I agreed
—this was before I started writing these pages—to do my
quota of going around to foundations and soliciting their
financial aid.

About foundations, my feelings are mixed, since I suspect they can never, however wisely administered, make
up for the damage which was done by collecting the money
in the first place. However, like most women, I seldom
experience much difficulty in choosing between two evils.
(This shady dexterity may account for the fact that the
female sex has never produced any great philosophers—a
charge which has always seemed to me inconclusive, to say
the least.) At any rate, the Negro high-school students were
there, and I was enthusiastic about their going on to college.

I did not loathe soliciting foundations because I am
ambivalent about foundations. I loathed it because a feature of my youth—only oldsters will remember this—was

something called "refinement." "Refined" people are supposed to be utterly above anything coarse and mundane like money—at least, if they are women. Especially, they are not supposed to go around with their hats in their hands, begging for it. Logically considered, this is nonsense; but it is nonsense I learned when I was rather young for logic.

I was completely unnerved by the prospect of approaching the foundations. But I did it, and I failed at it. The organization did get money from foundations; but not from any of the ones solicited—in a manner not noticeably suggestive of Richard Coeur d'Lion—by me. Nevertheless, in terms of the moral effort involved, I am quite sure that if St. Peter ever gives me a starry crown, it will say on the front, "She asked for money." If St. Peter is truly an angel, he will not add, "P.S. She did not get it."

The Do-Gooders do not enjoy their job, but the significant thing—and this is very important—is that they did not expect to enjoy it. About the pleasures of virtuous conduct, they were "disillusioned" when they were little toddlers attending Sunday School. And therein lies a difference between our two societies which it is of paramount importance to grasp. The Judeo-Christian ethic does not promise people freedom from pain. American business, however, does. And, obviously, that is a promise it cannot keep. The business society promises the businessman—the promise is implicit in practically every line uttered by the communications industry—that if he will just follow the club rules, he will either arrive at emotional maturity by magic, or he will be so happy and powerful in buying things and pushing people around that he will enjoy having his boyhood extend to the brink of the grave.

It is because of this false promise that I do not look to see the American business society last as long as Ancient Egypt or dynastic China. If one puts aside, for the moment, all the tribal myths and legends about American business—if one looks at American business with the eye of a visitor from another planet—the most conspicuous thing about it is that nobody likes it. "Everybody's out for the fast buck," says the man in the street, and his manner does not convey that he thinks this is a good thing. It is unlikely, though, that the business society as we know it today will be destroyed by the insurgent peasantry. People without risk capital do not care enough about business to destroy it. People with no prospect of being successful American businessmen—and this includes the majority of employees, as well as women and artists— would be happy if business would pick up its marbles and go away. But their underlying attitude toward business is less one of hostility than of indifference.

There are only two possible future developments for the American business society. It can either destroy itself in blood and flame—dropping atom bombs on Chinese cities would be a handy way to start this process—or it can modulate into a "welfare state" with a philosophy of government sufficiently well-rounded to exorcise the much—and rightly —dreaded specter of regimentation. (Of the philosophy of government, in terms of the anti-business America, more

will be said later.) However, if the American business society is destroyed, it will be destroyed from the top and not
from the bottom. It will not be destroyed by schoolchil-
dren who have been subverted by collectivist textbooks. It
will be destroyed by angry businessmen who—promised
freedom from pain and not getting it—put their arms
around the pillars of the temple, like Samson, and avenge
themselves the hard way.

My own experience of being a do-gooder was lonely,
dismal and frightening; but I would nevertheless make
the same choices over again without a moment's hesita-
tion. Whatever their drawbacks, those decisions gave me
a sense of there being some continuity between my father's
life and mine. They gave me a feeling of having roots in
the past—the distant past as well as the immediate past.
To try to get through life without that feeling, especially
if one has children, is to suffer a much deeper and more
permanent anxiety than anything a do-gooder has to experience. I have not made anything like the amount of
money that, with my lucky start, I could have made; and
for that reason I am considered, by some few of my acquaintances and relatives, a disappointing failure. But my
daughter does not currently share this view, and I have a
cheerful suspicion that she never will.

X

Men, Women, and Children Last

————

THE *hearts of small children are delicate organs. A cruel beginning in this world can twist them into curious shapes. The heart of a child can shrink so that forever afterward it is hard and pitted as the seed of a peach. Or again, the heart of such a child may fester and swell until it is a misery to carry within the body, easily chafed and hurt by the most ordinary things.*

These words were not culled from a book on child care, though they might well have been. They are from the pen of the gifted novelist, Carson McCullers. But they certainly express—although more poetically and powerfully than is usually the case—something that all conscientious parents have had drilled into them.

A business society is embarrassingly well supplied with peach-pit hearts. But before condemning out of hand the mothers and fathers who produced the peach-pit hearts, the point must be made—again and again—that responsible, compassionate parenthood in an Upward Step commonwealth is an astonishingly difficult job. There is small reason to wonder that it is sometimes done badly. A cruel beginning in this world need not mean anything as obvious as being beaten up by a drunken father. A cruel beginning in this world is not incompatible with the best of care. The best of care can be given mechanically, and can serve as a screen—to everyone but the child—for a basic preoccupation, as per instructions, with getting ahead. The best of care can be nothing more than an elaborate system of defensive and escape buying.

All parents are familiar with the small child's command, "Pay attention to me!" But to pay *real* attention to children, in a business-dominated society, is sometimes just not humanly possible. Children's demands for affection and attention are vigorous and unremitting—at least, until they learn better—but these demands often land with a screech on parental nerves tightened apprehensively against the heartless atmosphere of profit-making. The new and compelling doctrine of child-raising is that we should be permissive with our children. But who is going to be permissive with the parents? Certainly not American business.

The tightened nerves of American parents are going to have a very considerable bearing on the future destiny of the United States. Since there is no possibility of persuading the children to demand less, the only way to make the

American destiny fruitful and life-giving, instead of destructive and death-dealing, is to cope with the problem of relaxing the parental nerves. If one listens to Official Dogma, this job is hopeless. According to Official Dogma, the parental nerves are being frayed and rubbed raw by people over whom we have no control—to wit, the undeniably hostile Russians.

But there is ground for the suspicion that in some of the contemporary expertizing about Russia, we are not so much looking at the Russians, as we are looking away from ourselves. The great disadvantage of looking away from ourselves is that it turns parenthood into one long series of instrument landings. In pursuit of a little more visibility for American fathers and mothers, it might be a constructive notion to give the Russians a rest for a moment and to study with a meditative eye the three primary character traits which American business has set up as the hallmark of the good human being—aggression, competitiveness and skepticism.

Of the three, competitiveness needs the most extended treatment. Speaking simply as a parent, I am not at all sure that I want to see my little girl develop a highly competitive personality. I am even less sure that she will have a good life if she marries someone with a highly competitive personality. But competitiveness is celebrated by American business as a desirable and socially creative quality. Men striving against each other, the theory goes, get more things done, and do them better, than men who are working simply because the job itself gives them self-respect.

But if competitiveness is socially creative, what does it create? The answer that it creates money and machines—the two great commodities most closely linked with the name of the United States—will probably not be open to much dispute. The machines are a real achievement. They are our great national contribution to human welfare, and we have a right to be proud of them. But there is a possibility that we are not quite so much indebted to American competitiveness for these machines as we usually assume.

The great Greek plays which have come down to us through the ages were the result of a public competition among contemporary playwrights, so it may fairly be allowed that competitiveness plays a certain role in creative activity—whether it involves machinery or plays. But a competition is always *for* something. It always has a goal, and the most significant part of the competition is the nature of the goal. The goal of the Greek competitions was to inspire plays which would give the population a healthy emotional purge. The goal of American competitiveness is to make money. The machines—highly creditable as they are, in terms of human welfare—were a by-product. Machines make markets, and markets make money. The goal of American competitiveness is not machinery for other men's aching backs. The goal of American competitiveness is money for one's own aching heart.

229

The Greek competitions were designed to benefit a great many people. The goal of that competitiveness was religious, communal and social. The goal of American competitiveness is individualistic, personal, non-co-operative and self-seeking. It is "private" enterprise in every sense of the word—my foot on the other fellow's neck. If proof is needed that American competitors aim to make money for themselves rather than to produce machinery for the benefit of everyone, one has only to consider that TVA is the rather lonely example in the United States of the use of machinery—by itself, and divorced from profit-making —to mitigate human toil. There are half a dozen other areas in the country where similar projects could have a similarly magnificent effect in raising the standard of living, but TVA just barely squeaked past the hostility of American business, and it took the tragic, criminally wasteful and totally unnecessary floods of last spring to reactivate even the mention of a Missouri Valley Authority.

American machinery is not the conscious and deliberate expression of the national genius, as were the Greek plays. It is the inadvertent by-product of American competition for money. This circumstance accounts for the fact that although the machines are the glory of our society, we do not enjoy them very much. In their entirety, they make us nervous. Although the machines are supposed to belong to the Americans, they are often spoken of as if it were the other way around. Actually, we are not the slaves of our machines, since machines do not have the capacity for enslavement. We are the slaves of *what the machines are used for*. We are the prisoners of money.

Competitiveness is, in essence, a special way of looking at one's fellow human beings. One does not look at them carefully and interestedly, in order to see what they are really like. One merely keeps glancing at them nervously in order to make sure, if they are behind, that they stay behind, or, if they are ahead, that the gap is being closed up. The basis of competitiveness is permanent insecurity. And permanent insecurity—no matter how much it can, and sometimes does, produce in the way of expanded income—makes the job of rearing children a disguised little purgatory for all concerned.

The disadvantage of competitiveness, as a social force, is that it cannot be contained within the limits of office and factory. It spills out into non-business areas. Is your child more "secure" than mine? Does your daughter have more dates than my daughter? Do you keep a cleaner kitchen, do a whiter wash, play a better bridge game or carry your liquor better than I do? It does not matter whether we are liked; but we *must* be envied. Competitiveness is sanctified unrest; but upon unresting people —no matter how thrice-blessed they are by American business—the demands of children are a heavy drain.

American competitiveness, as fostered and encouraged by the business society, does actually serve a social function. But not a good one. In an industrial society, much of the work which has to be done is monotonous, boring and depersonalized. A housewife—if she wants to take the trouble, and if she is living above the subsistence level—can put the stamp of her personality upon her dwelling place. Upon her children, too, for that matter. But short of throwing sand into the machinery, there is nothing the worker on an assembly line can do to distinguish his work from that of the man next to him. A file clerk cannot personalize filing except by doing it badly.

Nor is this depersonalization of work limited solely to the lower echelons of industry. Frederick Wakeman in *The Hucksters* and Eric Hodgins in *Blandings' Way* have given us a graphic picture of sterile occupations among the top brass. Apropos of the question posed in Chapter I—What is the real nature of American life, as distinguished from the various popular legends?—it is extremely important to keep in mind that American business can sometimes be just as boring for those who are well paid as for those who are not.

In this situation, competitiveness—at all income levels—serves the purpose of displacing attention from the work itself and focusing it instead upon the other workers. This sounds as if it might be a good thing. But attention is not directed to the other workers for purposes of warmth, friendship and shared endeavor in a deeply felt cause. The other workers are not friends or co-idealists, but antagonists upon whom it is necessary to keep an Argus eye. By injecting this note of personal struggle into business activity, a certain amount of artificial excitement is created, in spite of the fact that some of that activity is quite the opposite of exciting. But the excitement is synthetic. It does not touch people's hearts. And after a while it leaves them empty, cheated, disillusioned and ready to drop atom bombs on other hemispheres just for the sake of having one single moment of feeling really alive.

Some of our bolder social thinkers have made the extremely sensible suggestion that since a certain amount of boring work is unavoidable in a highly mechanized society, people should be paid a living wage for doing it no more than three hours a day—leaving the rest of their time free for activities about which they are able to feel a little genuine enthusiasm. This suggestion, so far from being Utopian, is a much more practical approach to "human nature" than the feverish myth that in an industrial society, all the work is challenging. We are kept from putting such an approach into practice, not by the fact that our machines are unequal to it—they are more than equal to it—but by the fact that we have gotten so accustomed to being bored that it seems natural to us. We hug our chains. A bored population, however, is a potentially dangerous population.

The most damaging charge against competitiveness is that it wreaks havoc with the parent-child relationship. The child is his parents' "product." He is good or bad, accepted or rejected, in terms of how he stacks up with the other "products." Since there is no definite ideal of what constitutes a good human being—especially where children are concerned, for children do not have the escape hatch of being successful businessmen—the mothers and fathers have to keep looking, not only at their own child, but also at the child ahead and the child behind.

One of the things by which I was most struck, during the year when I was teaching, was how competitive the parents were and how thirstily grateful they would have been for some clear-cut and reasonably attainable standard of merit by which to set their compasses. The dominant society gives us a clear-cut standard—making a lot of money —but most of us cannot meet the standard, and it is impossible to use it with children.

What does American competitiveness mean, in terms of the child himself? It means that the child never knows when some other child will turn up whose performance he will be expected to beat. This can certainly be defined, within the meaning of the act, as a cruel beginning in this world. At best, life is an uncertain and intermittently tragic proposition, and men have never found any way of responding to it adequately except by trying to understand their fellow men. Competitiveness, however, reduces human companionship to a set of space relationships. How far ahead? How far behind? How cold and lonely!

The other two qualities which the business society nurtures and applauds—aggression and skepticism—are somewhat different in nature from competitiveness. They are not, in themselves, either good or bad. Their merit or lack of merit depends on the uses to which they are put. In business societies, the goal of aggression is money; but aggression is capable of being put to much broader use than that. To drive the money-changers out of the Temple was indisputably an aggressive act. In fact, it was accomplished with a whip.

Similarly, skepticism in a business society finds its usual expression in the belief that human beings are incapable of idealism—at least, until they have first established themselves as successful businessmen. But skepticism, although we are most familiar with it in the role of handmaiden to business, can with equal facility be turned against business. It can be used to set us free from the business myths and financial legends which are choking the life out of the American spirit.

That the American population has been intensively trained to be aggressive and skeptical is not in itself a disastrous state of affairs. The possibility of disaster does not lie in these characteristics themselves. Actually, they can be very useful and satisfying qualities to have, *provided they have a goal which is big enough to contain them*. But the making of money is not such a goal. It is too small a target to accommodate the aggression and skepticism of the American population and to leave that population healthily tired, relaxed and satisfied. Just as it is not our machines in themselves which are bad, but the fact that we use them for the basically trivial purpose of making sales—so it is not aggression and skepticism which are harmful, but the fact that money-making is not a big enough purpose to exhaust them. There is a dangerous residue left over. The decent people bottle up this residue and punish themselves. They suffer from insomnia and other forms of anxiety. The indecent people do not bottle it up. They punish others.

If the making of money is not a large enough goal to use up our national energy, what goal is large enough? At the risk of setting the obedient, unquestioning American somewhat back on his heels, the suggestion is advanced that the much-derided objective of "making the world a better place" will absorb all the aggression and skepticism anyone can put into it, and there will still be room left over. The aggressive man who drove the money-changers out of the Temple was not blighted by the Five O'Clock Shadow which casts its pall of pressure and suffering over so much of American life. The career of Christ shows periodic evidence of hostile behavior, but it was not *surplus* hostility. He used the hostility. It did not use Him. The people who clamor for a preventive war furnish a sad example of human beings who are not the managers of their own aggressiveness, but its victims.

"Making the world a better place" can take any one of a thousand forms. It may take the form of permanently improving children's bodies through Federal funds for hot school lunches. It may take the form of permanently increasing the productivity of men and meadowlands through projects like TVA. The list could be multiplied indefinitely, but the phrase speaks for itself. To the people who have had the experience, in however small a way, of leaving the world better than they found it, the idea will not be wholly unfamiliar or unrecognizable. The people who have never wished to have that experience are unlikely to see these pages. The supreme importance of "making the world a better place" is that—so far from being a laughable and "unrealistic" goal—it is the only objective broad enough to take the impact of the aggression and skepticism which have been implanted in the American character. To try to use the American personality, in the present stage of its development, for as flimsy a goal as money-making is like trying to put a Diesel engine into a baby carriage.

If children are to get the affection they need, the tightened nerves of American parents will have to be examined with a view to remedial measures, and not just accepted with a sigh as the cross we have to bear. American life is so energetic and so seething with activity that it is difficult to pierce through the agitated surface and see the unsatisfied cravings lying underneath. But unless those cravings can be acknowledged and—to a certain extent, at least—satisfied, it is a waste of time to talk about children needing love. Children need love, but they are by no means the only people who need it.

On the score of taut parental nerves, there is one circumstance which—though not generally recognized or very frequently discussed—is pivotal. The circumstance is that, except as a consumer, the child-bearing and child-rearing woman is of no use to the business society. To be sure, were I not a woman, I would not have the temerity to be writing this book. The business society is fundamentally indifferent to, and unaware of, women. Hence it permits the American female to display an interest in ethics and morality for which an American male would be razed to the ground like Carthage. The English anthropologist, Geoffrey Gorer, refers at some length—in his book, *The American People*—to American women as the carriers and transmitters of American morality. The "nihilistic progress" (of American business)—says Mr. Gorer—"is held back by the tightly corseted figure of Madame Chairman, by the pinched and overeager schoolmarm. They are the present embodiments of the Goddess of Liberty." *

In a business society, there are only two things the maternal woman can do, and both of them are bad. She can try to get closer to the male by taking on, to a certain extent, the supposedly male characteristics of aggressiveness, competitiveness and skepticism. A reminder should perhaps here be inserted of something already said. It is not necessary actually to be in business to have an aggressive, competitive and skeptical approach to other human beings. One can have a primitive, tribal and childlike belief in the magical power of money without actually earning money.

If the child-rearing woman in the business society is unable or unwilling to be a sort of echo of the business world, then her only other choice is to live out her life in a lonely trance. The American woman's day is customarily so full of activity and so crammed with duties and obligations that it may seem odd to speak of her as either lonely or tranced. But the very absence of leisure—the very absence of any time for laziness and meditation—suggests a flight

---

* Mr. Gorer is a somewhat waspish commentator, but the present writer is not in a very strong position to tax a British subject with lack of charity.

from pain. The source of the pain is that the maternal woman is rejected by the business society.

Activities she has in abundance, but they have no status and no prestige. The child-rearing woman in the business-dominated United States can keep busy until she drops in her tracks, but she is still "just a housewife." She does not "work"; she does not produce "results"; and she has never met a payroll. Fourteen thousand different ways will be invented to persuade her to buy Washing Machine A instead of Washing Machine B. The fact that it would be possible for her to have a washing machine without any wasteful and meaningless scuffle called "free competition" will be noted by nobody except her own subconscious.* She may rely with a good deal of certainty on receiving a gift on Mother's Day, but the one thing she may *not* have—she and all her ilk—is another TVA.

This is not sexual chauvinism, although it may sound like it at first blush. If it is chauvinism at all, it is human-race chauvinism. I am not angry because the Overbearing Males of the business society have denied maternal women the respect and prestige to which they are entitled. Rather, I am concerned because the Overbearing Males—insofar as they support and believe in a business society—are inad-

---

* It will, of course, be argued that owing to "free competition," the maternal woman can get Washing Machine A twenty dollars cheaper than Washing Machine B. It is the tiniest of blessings. The maternal woman does not pay merely for the cost of putting the washing machine together, plus a modest profit. She pays for the advertising, the public relations, the expense account and the house organ. Into each washing machine some Martinis must fall.

vertently robbing themselves. The counterpart of the maternal woman is the paternal man. But in our business-dominated Republic, the paternal man is not allowed to come into existence until the sunset gun. This is, to say the least, rather late in the day. What keeps the human race going—what guarantees its fullest and richest development—is not money and machines, but maternal women and paternal men. If American women are amateurish and ineffective in their concern with ethics and morality—and it must be honestly admitted that they are—the difficulty is that the job is too big for a single sex. The Ethics Department is understaffed.

The child-bearing and child-rearing woman can echo business attitudes and admire business goals—and to the extent that she does so, she is unfeminine and unmotherly. If she cannot echo and admire, she is isolated and immobilized. In either case, her ability to give her children real, and not mechanical attention is gravely impaired. Love, affection, tenderness, sympathy and compassion are not qualities which the individual, all by himself, *invents*. They are qualities that he *transmits*. The qualities which make a woman maternal are condemned by American business as "idealistic" and "impractical." The maternal woman in the contemporary United States is therefore in the position of trying to give her children something she is not receiving herself. It *can* be done—just barely—by extremely determined people. American middle-class parents are, for the most part, extremely determined people. They have to be. But a society which puts parents under this kind of strain has very little chance of lasting for a thousand years.

By the Freudian psychoanalysts, the unsatisfied cravings which lie beneath the hurried, unresting, hyperactive surface of American life are described as a yearning for physiological sex. But this is an oversimplification. The yearning —the unsatisfied craving—is there. But it is not a yearning for the act of sex. It is a yearning for an atmosphere—an unbusinesslike atmosphere of generosity and ease and sanctioned idealism and wide spiritual horizons. In such an atmosphere, physiological sex would be, for a great many people, both reliable and rewarding. This kind of atmosphere has, of course, one serious drawback. In that kind of emotional and moral climate, nobody could make a nickel out of sex.

The so-called "women's magazines"—in a sincere and genuine attempt to be helpful—devote a good deal of space to American marriage problems. But these well-intentioned articles are usually wide of the mark. The difficulty is not, as the magazine writers say, that American males and American females have had an inadequate training in how to get along with each other. The difficulty is that American males and American females have had an inadequate training in how to get along with *anybody*. They are competitive. Billions and billions of dollars have been spent to make them that way. They are money-oriented— for the extremely sensible reason that they have seen with their own eyes what happens to people in the United States who are not money-oriented.

241

To be fully male or fully female means to be paternal or maternal. Animals are capable of siring. Only human beings are capable of fatherhood. There is a curious paradox about mid-century American life which I think will be more apparent to my daughter and her contemporaries —when they grow up—than it is to us. Despite the romantic movies, the titillating advertisements, the bosomy comics and the concupiscent popular fiction, the American business society is sexless. It is not a male society. It is a neuter society. That is one of the principal reasons why so many people do not like it. That is why it cannot be relied upon to last very long.

Another factor which tightens the nerves of American parents is the emphasis placed on that ill-assorted cluster of attitudes known as American foreign policy. It is one of the fictions of American life that American foreign policy has a special and separate kind of importance. In the editorials and the think-pieces, foreign policy seems to be suspended, like Mohammed's coffin, between earth and heaven. However, American foreign policy is not, and never can be, anything more than domestic policy for export. It needs to be administered by specially talented, gifted or experienced people only to the extent that domestic policy also needs to be administered by such people.

The human beings on this planet are organized into various societies, and almost all these societies are currently in flux and in torment. It cannot be said that the American press—concerned, as it has to be, with salable facts—plays down this turbulence. Or knows how to in-

terpret it. But American behavior toward these other societies—"free" or not "free"—is not hard to explain.

Each of our two American societies would like to capture American foreign policy. Not only would each of
them like to. Each of them has. We have Point Four, and
we have the isolationists. We have the Marshall Plan, and
we have the bold spirits who want to reduce everything to
beautiful simplicity by dropping atom and hydrogen
bombs on Russia.

One thing may be said with certainty about American
foreign policy. It is honest. It reflects with mirrorlike ex-
actitude the split in the American personality. Our foreign
policy owes some of its seeming importance to the fact that
it provides—or seems to provide—a wonderful excuse for
not facing up to the headaches of domestic policy. But
those headaches somehow manage to wangle a visa and slip
past the Statue of Liberty anyway. The sustained note in
all the discussions of American foreign policy is the note
of exasperation. Americans are not really interested in foreign policy, for the quite understandable reason that they
have too many troubles at home. Literally at home—in
their dwelling places. When the maternal woman and the
paternal man must constantly apologize to business for existing, they can scarcely be expected to have much sympathy for the woes of peasants six thousand miles away.

The best remedy for the tightened nerves of American
parents is perspective. A good deal is said and written in
the United States about the Russians dropping atom
bombs on New York, and since my little girl's father works

in that metropolis, it is a topic to which I am disposed to pay serious attention. But while the Russians have been consistently abusive, arrogant, vituperative and dismayingly non-middle-class, they have never threatened to bomb us. If they had, we may be sure the American communications industry would have let us know. It would be *the* salable fact of the day.

In terms of perspective, it is of the utmost importance to realize that both American business and Russian Communism are materialistic societies based on the idea that man is primarily an economic animal. Where they differ is in their separate approaches to this economic-ness. The Judeo-Christian ethic, on the other hand, asserts that man is *not* primarily an economic animal. According to that ethic, man manipulates economics—not vice versa—and he manipulates them, moreover, with his eye fixed on non-economic, brotherly, co-operative and nonmaterialistic goals.

American business is hostile to Russia because the Russian state, though materialistic, is a non-money society. The anti-business America is hostile to Russia because it is a cruel, arbitrary and nonhumanitarian state. Could not the two American societies pool their interest and form a common front against Russia? The answer is no. American business asserts that money, while not everything, comes first. Christian morality avers that any conclusions based on this premise are false and essentially unworkable. The two American societies have their *separate* reasons for being opposed to Russia, and it is utterly impossible to combine these two separate reasons.

The Big Fight of our time is not going to come. It has come. The tightened nerves of American parents are partly due to the fact that we are all despairingly apprehensive of a planet-destroying conflict between the United States and the U.S.S.R. This apprehension, if justifiable, makes the job of trying to turn children into good human beings somewhat academic, to say the least. However, this Titanic struggle has not yet taken place. But under cover of the threat, an equally Titanic struggle actually is taking place, and that is the conflict between the quickly evolving American business society and our two-thousand-year-old morality. This internal struggle is infinitely and supremely the more important—if for no other reason than that it is not still in the future. It is occurring right now.

Most Americans are conscious of this desperate subterranean conflict only through the panicky awareness that old, familiar landmarks have disappeared. Mr. Whittaker Chambers—whose life has at no time suggested the reserved, self-reliant, self-disciplining Puritan—is enshrined as a responsible man and a reliable witness. Senator McCarthy is regarded by respectable Americans with horror, but if there is one thing in the world about which the Senator from Wisconsin is cheerful and undismayed, it is the wrath of respectable Americans.

In the supposedly sacred name of foreign policy—and to insure that the clinkers left over from the holocaust will be American clinkers—a great many of our old, familiar landmarks of proper behavior and recognized decency have been done away with. But there is only one really significant aspect of American foreign policy at the present time, and that is how clearly it shows that it is time for us angels to look homeward. "I will not turn my back on Alger Hiss" was not "policy"; but to a great many middle-aged and/or middle-class Americans, it was not foreign, either.

XI

The Consent of the Governed

ASHLAND, OHIO, June 9 (AP)—Senator Robert A. Taft, Republican, of Ohio, in a commencement address at Ashland College here today, advised the eighty-seven graduates to avoid government work as a career. Civil service jobs, he said, in his commencement address, offer little opportunity for advancement.

New York Herald-Tribune
June 10, 1950

* * *

GOVERNMENT ATTORNEYS

Editor
New York Herald-Tribune
New York, New York

Dear Sir:

In your editorial column you have posed the rhetorical question: "But when a businessman, a corporation or an income-tax payer is involved, what government lawyer ever stops to worry about fairness?"

At first blush, such a question would appear to be libelous per se to any member of the bar who has chosen to make a career of public service rather than to represent the corporations, businessmen or income-tax payers for whom you are apparently so solicitous.

I have been a "government lawyer" for fifteen years, engaged in Admiralty and other aspects of the maritime law for the United States, both at home and abroad. I have always deemed it a privilege and honor to be so employed by the United States, although, I might add to you, as a "taxpayer," at considerable personal financial loss. You probably could not understand the motives which have prompted me to so serve my country, for your editorial indicates that you believe all government attorneys are unethical knaves. However, I sincerely believe that the government of the United States, of which you and I are a component part, vitally requires the services of experienced attorneys to insure that all of us receive equal protection under the law.

My return inquiry to you is: "Did you stop to think about fairness when you published such a canard about all government lawyers?"

> Frederick K. Arzt
> Member, National Republican Club
> Baltimore, Md.
> March 17, 1950

The two men quoted above are both Republicans and they are both government employees. But in their attitudes toward American government—and, indeed, toward life itself—they are poles apart.

American government is a topic very close to this writer's heart, since I was brought up in a Civil Service household. There is no part of my little girl's social heritage which is potentially more comforting or more fortifying than the American system of representative government; but there is also no part of that inheritance which is more sadly in need of having fact dug out from the obscuring fiction. The American child gets accustomed at a very early age to hearing government brushed off as "politics"—polluted, cynical and too unashamedly venal for decent people to be involved with. This popular and widely held notion is not so much inaccurate or untrue, as it is out of focus.

Few people would be prepared to quarrel with the statement that Senator Taft defends and champions the business society. In that role, he unwittingly—and with complete sincerity—reveals the basically anarchistic quality of the business community. If all the young people agreed with Senator Taft about the paramount importance of "advancement," who would teach the children to read and write? Who would deliver the mail? Who would administer justice in the courts?

This book has no villains, and the Senator's commencement speech has not been disinterred with the idea of making the gentleman from Ohio look like the Prince of Darkness. Senator Taft is non-regal, and does not figure in people's minds as any kind of prince at all. In both the Democratic and Republican parties, there are public figures whose actions and fairly consistent policies quite recognizably have their roots in a sense of morality. In both parties, there are equally identifiable, and infinitely more numerous, public figures who break lances on behalf of business as wholeheartedly as Senator Taft. Senator Taft is distinguished from the other business-minded legislators (of both parties) only by a certain stark and tundralike simplicity for which one must, in the last analysis, be grateful. He is not a talk-gooder.

In a split society, what happens to representative government? The embittered query of the *Herald-Tribune* editorial writer—Where business is concerned, what government official ever stops to be fair?—reflects a widely prevalent feeling in the business community that government is hostile to business. The question of fairness has been adequately disposed of by the correspondent from Maryland, but the feeling of the business community is quite correct. Representative government *is* hostile to business.

In our country, there is a basic clash between government and business. Government cannot be anarchistic and irresponsible, and still be government. Business, on the other hand—with its emphasis on private financial triumph as the first and most important job of any human being—cannot be anything except anarchistic and irresponsible, as Senator Taft so truly, if unintentionally discloses. The middle-aged businessman—his pile safely made—is sometimes prepared to relax and to take a genuine interest in the fortunes of unbusinesslike people. But what can he do about the younger men who are still remorselessly and ruthlessly on their way up? Or about older ones who never arrive at relaxation at all?

The desirability of co-operation between government and business is a favorite topic of American editorial writers. However, the nature of representative government and the nature of American business are such that there never has been any co-operation between them and there never will be. The business community sometimes permits the government to underwrite the losses on railroads, transatlantic liners or mail-carrying airlines. It never willingly cuts the government in on the profits from such enterprises. Such a policy falls a little short of co-operation.

In our time, it has become a function of government to take care of the unbusinesslike minorities in those areas where they cannot take care of themselves. It is the old frontier pattern of protection of the weak. For the purpose of protecting the weak, the government uses funds, a portion of which the American Do-Gooders have wrenched and pried loose from the business society. It is not possible for the government, if it is to remain a representative government, to yield to business' stern demand that the unbusinesslike minorities should be forced to become businesslike or be made to take the consequences.

Since American business is the dominant one of our two societies, it is sometimes able to capture government; but capture is not the same thing as co-operation. When the government succeeds in evading capture—as it did, to a large extent, under Franklin Roosevelt—its relationship with the business community is, and has to be, one of incurable struggle. In our torn-down-the-middle Republic, the same thing happens to government which happens to the Judeo-Christian ethic. Government is spoken of by the communications industry with the highest respect, until it goes into action on behalf of the unbusinesslike. When it goes into action to protect the weak, and thereby *becomes* a government, the respect is instantly transmuted into derision, contempt and hostility.

But American representative government is, by definition, supposed to do one thing. It is supposed to represent. Most of the people in the United States are unbusinesslike —and will continue to be, until the Last Trump. Hence it is the unbusinesslike people who ought to have the most influence on the American government, and whose needs and potentialities that government should be most concerned with. In these pages, I have avoided like the plague any use of the word "democracy." That beat-up collection of sinned-against syllables has taken such a mauling that it is no longer possible for any two Americans to agree on what they mean by it. Everybody, however, knows what is meant by representative government.

Against the American representative government, two accusations have been consistently and unceasingly leveled by the business community. These two accusations have been so staunchly reiterated that almost everybody believes them—even, sometimes, government people themselves. The first accusation is that our representative gov-

ernment is inefficient. The second accusation is that that
government is inevitably and innately corrupt.

The idea that American business is efficient and American government is inefficient has been so relentlessly
dinned into our ears that to question it verges on blasphemy. However, this year's blasphemy is next year's liberating truth; and the fact of the matter is that efficiency
in itself is meaningless. Efficiency has no importance except in connection with what one is being efficient *about*.
Indisputably, American business is efficient; but according to the findings of the Kefauver Committee, American
crime is even more efficient than American business. At
least, that is what it said in the papers.

It is a mistake to accept meekly and without query the
legend that American representative government is a con-
temptible clump of dim-witted bureaucrats tied up like a
Schrafft's Week-end Special in yards of red tape. The sacri-
legious but not wholly unpalatable fact remains that never
since it emerged in recognizable form—not even during
the Civil War—has the American government cracked up,
gone to pieces and failed in its job of governing the way
the business society cracked up, went to pieces and failed
in its job of being prosperous in 1929. This may be treason, but by all means let us make the most of it. It is one of
the most stabilizing and reassuring facts in the whole of
American life.

Historically, American government has been more efficient than American business, and for this demonstrable

superiority, there is a sound reason. Our population has always, fortunately, included a certain number of Americans who wanted the working years of their lives to add up to something better than three or four decades of self-seeking. In terms of government employment, this kind of American antedates the New Deal by a good long time and can by no means be uniformly relied upon to approve of Franklin D. Roosevelt and his works. When this kind of public servant receives any attention at all, it is generally unfavorable. There is hardly a newspaper in the country which would not automatically allude to the government lawyer quoted above as a "bureaucrat." According to the dictionary, a bureaucrat is "an official who works by fixed routine without exercising intelligent judgement." The bureaucrat's letter, however, is almost embarrassingly superior in intelligence and discernment to Senator Taft's awkward little effort at vocational guidance.

The strength and staying power of American government are based on, an idea. This idea the lawyer from Maryland has expressed with a certain amount of eloquence—to wit, that it is an honor and a privilege to serve the United States, even at the cost of a certain amount of "advancement." About this idea, there is one really superlative attribute. It does not have to be abandoned at five o'clock. The owner can—with complete propriety and utter safety—bring it home from the office. It does not do the children a bit of harm.

Behind the charge that American government is inefficient lies the tacit assumption that that government is a

money-making organization which has somehow disgrace-
fully failed to make money. Which has done even worse—
which has lost money. However, government in the United
States is not, and cannot be, a money-making institution.
Government renders a great many services to people who
cannot pay for them. Children, for example. (Indeed—in
the form of favorable legislation—it also renders services to
people who could pay for them, but do not want to. Stockholders, for instance, in luminously non-anemic indus-
tries.) In the United States, American business and representative government cannot *both* make money. It has to
be one or the other.

Government is not business. It is wholly different in motive and intent from business. Business is unashamedly individualistic and self-seeking. The social scientists have a
special word for it. They call it "privatist." Government,
on the other hand, is public, communal and concerned
with the welfare of all the citizens, and not just the ones
who are talented acquirers. Potentially, there is an enormous amount of satisfaction in being able to live out one's
life in a country with a representative government. But
the whole flavor and quality of the American representative government turn to ashes on the tongue, if one regards
that government as simply an inferior and rather second-
rate sort of corporation.

In this country, we have a phenomenon which is described by the conservative press and conservative businessmen as "government spending." The fires of hell do
not look more hideous and alarming to American business

255

than the disbursal of funds by the United States government. "Government spending," however—as the phrase is used by the business society—has a very narrow and particular meaning. It does not refer to government moneys which, through renegotiation contracts, find their way into the businessman's pocket. It refers to the government moneys which are used to benefit The Type That Fails To Make Money. "Government spending" does not mean *all* government spending. It means the expenditure of money on children, veterans, farmers who cannot singlehandedly cope with the Dust Bowl, Navajos, old people, the victims of technological unemployment, drug addicts, Point Four foreigners and housewives who use government bulletins in doing their home canning and home nursing.

In business terms, it is "inefficient" to spend money for the purpose of conferring benefits on unconscious do-gooders of The Type That Fails To Make Money. But in terms of representative government, such spending is not only efficient—it is the only claim the government has to call itself representative. In our society, money is constantly moving in a circle. It goes out of the consumer's pocket and into the producer's. Then, via taxes, it goes out of the producer's pocket and into the government's. From the government, it flows back to the consumer in the form of postal services, new roads, day nurseries for "working" mothers, forest conservation and—when the unbusinesslike people are having a lucky year—TVA.

In business terms, only one arc of this circle is "efficient." When the money flows out of the consumer's pocket and into the producer's, the producer is "efficient." But when the producer is taxed, the taxing agency is de scribed as bungling, greedy, inept and punitive. And when the tax money is spent on people who have never met a payroll and who do not get "results," this is "government spending" and the communications industry assures us with passion and fervor that we must vote for the candidates who have sworn to put a stop to it.

If the American representative government ever reaches a point where American business is prepared to commend it as efficient, that government will have become tyrannical and nonrepresentative. (Or American business will have changed so that its own mother would not know it.) There is comfort and reassurance to be derived from American life in the middle of the twentieth century, but that comfort and reassurance are only available to people who are prepared to take business myths and financial legends with a very considerable grain of salt. Last year my husband and I bought—and paid cash for—a washing machine of a widely known and widely celebrated brand. The machine which was delivered to us was defective. It took three months of letters, phone calls and stayings-at-home-for-re-pairmen-who-did-not-come before the illustrious gadget was finally put into working order.

The incident is tiny, but not untypical. If American business would do something completely unprecedented— if it would stop perpetually talking to the American housewife and spend ten minutes listening to her—it would find that under many a $7.98 seersucker wrap-around lies a mute but stubborn skepticism about the allegedly flawless efficiency of the business society. When the American representative government takes three months to fix something which is broken, the blame is placed on red tape and bureaucratic inefficiency. When the American entrepreneur takes three months to fix something which is broken, nothing is said about red tape or inefficiency. When American business leans on its shovel—in the fashion so widely attributed to W.P.A. workers—the businessman has a rather lyrical name for the dawdling and delay. He calls it "the human factor."

The second charge which is constantly made against government—the charge that it is just naturally and inevitably corrupt—is not wholly untrue, but it needs to be brought into perspective. Corruption is a general circumstance of American life, and American government is very much a part of American life. Government officials sometimes take bribes. So do college athletes. However, the businessmen who offer the bribes do not do it out of sheer, wanton deviltry. They do it because they expect to make money faster by offering bribes than they could by not offering bribes. Between the little fellow's bribe and the big fellow's "fast deal," there is no essential difference. The bribe-taker and the bribe-giver both suffer from the common American blind spot. They are both unaware that money, over and above the simple needs of the flesh, does not solve problems—it just permits them to get worse.

In this present day and age, any talk of American government appears to lead quite naturally into the much-canvassed topic of loyalty to that government. Actually, this easy transition from the topic of government to the topic of loyalty is something which—the writer suspects—is not going to stand the test of time. Two or three decades from now, the American government will still be here (one imagines). But the next generation may not agree with those of their parents who said, in the middle of the century, that what keeps the government's chin above water is the informal crucifixions which take place in the name of discovering and punishing anti-government sentiments. To some Americans, those crucifixions do not look very handsome, even now; and Time is going to be merciless with them.

Before touching on the tangled subject of loyalty, it must be admitted that your correspondent is fully conscious that some of the viewpoints expressed in these pages may seem, at first glance, startling and unfamiliar. (Actually, the point of view herein contained is very, very old; and this book was put together with a Resurrector Set.) But the startling and unfamiliar can sometimes be extremely comforting; whereas the familiar—as we know it today—is disturbing, confusing and bleak. We have "public relations," "public opinion," "the power of the press" and all the din and racket of the all-too-communicative communications industry. But we also have—like Mr. Wordsworth's violet by the mossy stone—the sober truth.

Even by dogged pursuers, the sober truth is not very easily arrived at. But a good handy device for getting a line on it is to try to project one's self into the future and to imagine how contemporary attitudes and contemporary behavior are going to look to our children and grandchildren—as they reach maturity. When my father declined to change his name from Reinhold to Reginald, there were not lacking substantial and respected citizens who said he was giving aid and comfort to the enemy and that "traitor" was not too strong a word for him. (Of course, in that undeveloped era, everything was miniature and non-gigantic —even treason.) As time passed, however, the old man's testy negative came to look less and less like treason and more and more like the intelligent and rational action of a self-respecting citizen.

For my own part—since I have quite a stake in securing the good opinion of at least one member of the rising generation—the transmuting touch of time is something on which I like to keep a wary eye. Devoted and conscientious public servants like Mr. Seth W. Richardson, former Chairman of the President's Loyalty Review Board, have given extremely careful and painstaking study to the question of loyalty—or rather, to the question of disloyalty. Not for a moment do I wish to impugn the serious-mindedness of those mid-century Americans who have sincerely tried to come to grips with the issue in non-hysterical terms.

But one cannot help suspecting that in twenty or thirty years' time, the current obsession with loyalty is going to have its comic aspects. It is quite likely that the next generation will laugh out loud upon being told that a commonwealth whose official morality states categorically, "Thou shalt not bear false witness," was defended from its enemies (some people said) by Senator McCarthy. Over treason-by-letterhead and treachery-by-brother-in-law—otherwise known as guilt by association—our descendants will certainly chuckle. Was Christ a pickpocket because He was crucified between two thieves? The issue of loyalty or disloyalty to the United States can be considerably simplified by asking one brief question: Which United States? The American Way of Life can mean the anti-money, Jewish-Christian system of ethics which we have inherited from the distant past. Or it can mean the much-publicized and much-emphasized business philosophy that money, while not everything, comes first. *But it cannot mean both.*

The mid-century bacchanal about loyalty oaths and loyalty investigations and being "cleared" by this or that agency or smeared in a paroxysm of generalized spite has arisen out of a failure of understanding. What has not been understood is that to be anti-business does not ipso facto mean to be pro-Communist. Anti-business sentiments can stem from nothing more treacherous and unpatriotic than a thorough grounding in the principles of Christianity or Judaism. Presumably, libelers and self-servers can defend the American business society against Communism. At least, American business thinks they can. But libelers, self-servers and male and female hysterics cannot defend the American ethic against Russia—or even against Tierra del Fuego. It is a cardinal principle of the Judeo-Christian ethic that the end *never* justifies the means; and the evildoer does not exist to whom either our morale or our morality is the slightest bit indebted.

261

Except among trained social scientists—and not always among them—there is no recognition in the United States of the fact that we have a split society. This ignorance produces, every now and then, some paradoxical situations. The year before last, a great deal of money was spent on investigating the loyalty of two or three million Federal employees. Although government money was spent, the disbursal was not described as "government spending." Nobody, however, asked the pertinent question of what the Federal employees were supposed to be loyal *to*—to American business, which consigns government employees to the outer darkness of The Type That Fails To Make Money? Or to American representative government which, if it does not represent the interests of the unbusinesslike, is not representative at all?

Nothing exists by itself. Everything has roots in the past. The "treason" and "disloyalty" by which we have all been so much disturbed and so much puzzled have antecedents. Our problem, however, is that the communications industry—in giving what it describes as "coverage" to disloyal people—has presented us with salable facts instead of with the sober truth. A half-antecedent is as dangerous and misleading as a half-truth. A great many young Americans —my husband, for example, when he was nineteen—belonged briefly to the Young Communist League. According to current folklore, the most charitable interpretation of this bit of personal history would be that it was a hideous and disastrous mistake for which only a thousand strenuously vocal "mea culpas" can atone. However, what sets people free from American chronic anxiety is not salable facts or popular folklore. What clears the air and lets people breathe freely and untimorously again is the sober truth. The sober truth is that the precise moment in history when the Great Russian Experiment looked at its best also happened to be the precise moment in history when the American business society looked at its worst.

A young man might have joined the Young Communist League because he was angry and distressed at the undeserved misery which the Great Depression brought in its train. From immediate practical experience, he discovered that it is no more possible to team up Communism with the American ethic than it is possible to team up American business with the American ethic. But in terms of our ancient national morality—and those are the only terms which merit attention and respect—no apology is necessary for having made the discovery. It is not necessary to be sorry for not having a peach-pit heart.

Seen against its proper background of the needless waste and undeserved humiliation produced by the Great Depression, joining the Young Communist League was—if not *the* thing to have done—at least *one* of the things to have done. Betrayal was involved in the Great Depression; but it was the betrayal of harmless and hard-working Americans by a few self-willed and astigmatic business-lovers. Perspective and sober truth are the nearest things we have to a remedy for American chronic unhappiness. But perspective cannot be achieved without admitting that the Hoovervilles, the bread lines and the apple-sellers really existed. Because of them, some people committed suicide. Some people put on gray uniforms and pledged themselves to technocracy. And some people (by no means the least sensitive and least intelligent) turned—not so much toward Communism, as away from American business. The suicides are beyond anyone's reach. Technocracy is not making much headway in Asia. But the depression-inspired fellow travelers of the thirties—the depression-induced Communists of the thirties—are salable in just about the same way and just about the same direction as Uncle Tom was salable.

In the emotional vacuum which followed upon the end of World War II—a vacuum which was made emptier, even for the business society, by the death of President Roosevelt—a few ex-Communists turned back to the alabaster arms of American business and performed, for its sweet sake, prodigies of profitable peaching and remunerative talebearing. But a distinction must be made—merely in the sacred name of the human nervous system—between third-decade left-wingers who do not believe in human sacrifice and the very tiny, but highly publicized group of third-decade left-wingers who bandaged their bleeding hearts with other people's reputations.

I have mentioned the matter of long-dead Communist affiliation with a more or less prefatory purpose. In itself not particularly significant, it nevertheless raises a very important question. That question is: Why was it that, after the depression, a certain number of stable, rational and well-brought-up people thought—for a while—that they could discern in Communism the mien and lineaments of the Judeo-Christian ethic? Why has it been so scandalously easy for American business to pin the label of Communism on any sort of decent, humanitarian behavior?

The only possible answer appears to be that Communism and our ancient and traditional system of ethics seem to have something in common. And they do. The business society directs the individual's attention to himself. Furthermore, it urges him to cultivate and develop only those parts of his personality which he can sell. Both Communism and Western-world ethics, on the other hand, direct the individual's attention outward and away from himself. They both invite him to be subservient—in the literal sense of giving service, and of giving it under an agency which is postulated as bigger and more important than any single person's life.

Here, however, the resemblance ends. And very sharply. Communism directs the individual's attention toward the state; but state-worship is just as false an idol as money, and just as unworkable a substitute for the family. The Judeo-Christian ethic says that the state exists to serve man —not vice versa. It directs the individual's attention to what the theologically-minded call the Kingdom of God and what non-ritualists might be content to describe as the Kingdom Where Money Doesn't Count. Western-world morality directs man's attention to other men. These other men are conceived of—not as consumers or customers or competitors or expendable slaves of a governmental Moloch—but as complex, significant and valuable human

265

beings. Western-world morality, in short, directs man's attention to life itself.

The source of all our mid-century anxiety is supposed to be that we live in a two-piece world—the two pieces being Russian Communism and American democracy. But it is not a two-piece world; it is a three-piece world. For Americans, the three points of the triangle are Russian Communism, American business and American ethics. So far as the sober truth is concerned, there is nothing the Russians could do to us—or to anybody else, for that matter—which could not be parried by unashamed Judaism or entrenched Christianity, armed with our magnificent machines. A good many years ago, Franklin P. Adams summed up the American split society in one brilliant sentence—"Christmas is over, and business is business." When business is over and Christmas is Christmas, we shall have a good deal less reason to fear the Russians. What is even nicer, we shall have less reason to fear each other.

XII

Summary

———

SOMEWHERE in the United States a little boy is growing up who may some day ask for, and get, my daughter's hand in marriage. I think a good deal about that little boy. I wonder whether his mother is trying to escape from her essential loneliness, as a maternal woman in a business-dominated country, through an exhausting schedule of defensive and escape buying. I wonder whether his father is a successful businessman who—inarticulately oppressed by his job and baffled by his own character—cannot fully respond to the language of a child's face and body. Or perhaps his father is an unbusinesslike man whose courage and authority have been slowly but steadily eroded by the mechanical contempt of American business.

I wonder whether that little boy is going to school on part time, because a school board of "realistic" and "practical" men have concluded that it would be "government spending"—and unfair to the taxpayer—to construct new schools. I wonder whether the sensitive and intelligent schoolteachers who might have had a lasting and felicitous effect on his life—and therefore on my daughter's—have been driven out of the profession by distinctly lower-than-middle-class salaries. Or whether those teachers are constrained from giving him of their best because they know from harsh experience that their best will be described as "subversive."

In terms of Western-world morality, there is only one possible philosophy of parenthood, and that philosophy can be summed up fairly simply. It is impossible to betray another man's child—for whatever reason—without also betraying one's own. To do less than justice to another man's child, no matter who that man is, is to impair by that much the chances one's own children have for a life of meaning and purpose. This is the only—and the point should be emphasized, the *only*—rational, logical and realistic approach to "politics," to American government, to American business and, in short, to American life.

As these pages are being written, the American Congress has just voted down a proposal that the Federal government should command the income from tidelands oil and should use that revenue for the education of American children. "The halls of Congress"—in the words of one radio commentator—"are sweating and slippery with oil." It is the careless assumption of the business society that the only children who suffer from this kind of legislative behavior are the unimportant children of the un-businesslike. Actually, the oilmen's children, the lobbyists' children and the Congressional children were right in there taking the rap, too.

The mills of the gods grind slowly, but they grind exceeding small. A slippery inheritance is a disappointing inheritance and an unreliable inheritance. Thoughtless, myth-swallowing parents—no matter how well-heeled—produce anxious, unhappy children. And sometimes angry, defiant and rebellious children. Silk purses are made out of silk, and never out of porcine ears.

It is one of the most frequently reiterated fictions of American life that "private enterprise" is good for people and that everybody benefits from it, regardless of what his income is. Actually, "private enterprise" is not even good for the round pegs—the Dream Boys—the successful American businessmen. It amputates a section of the mind and heart which no human being really wants to relinquish. Furthermore, "private enterprise" leaks imperceptibly into the area of bringing up children. We bring up our children privately—as if, that is, there were no other children in the world. American children are as much personal adjuncts of the parent as the parent's bank account. Like the bank account, they must be fat and sassy, or the parent cannot be accounted "successful" as a parent. But "private enterprise" does not belong in the field of parenthood, and a society which springs this kind of leak is headed for something really drastic like death or reform.

American business—and the kind of legislation which

shields and protects it—is based on a theory which is never put into words, but which is often very successfully translated into action. That never-verbalized theory is that the American child has an obligation to the business society. His obligation consists of either (1) selecting for himself the kind of father who is able and willing to earn a good deal of money under circumstances which are frankly described as a rat race or (2) getting away from any other kind of father just as fast as a paper route can carry him.

Actually, of course, the grownups are responsible for the child—not vice-versa. Ideally—and in societies which survive and flourish, practically too—children learn to take responsibility in the same way they learn everything else which determines their cast of character and the kind of lives they ultimately live. Children learn to take responsibility by force of example. How much responsibility a child has learned to take—by the time he is grown up—depends on *the number of people who were able and willing to take responsibility for him.* Even if they did not know him personally. Even if he existed for them only as a statistic or a principle or a still-unrevealed son-in-law.

Children need love—not only from their own fathers and mothers—but also from all the other fathers and mothers in the society. Children need love, not only personally, but also *as a class.* Similarly, parents cannot do a good job in bringing up their children unless they, too, have status and prestige in their role of parents—regardless of whether they can or cannot make money. American children are the most important group of people, bar none, in the United States. The Americans who have been able to grasp that supremely decisive (if elusive) fact are identified in these pages as Do-Gooders. But they might with equal accuracy be described as the Children's Lobby.

The prevailing problem of the mid-century American is that he has a split personality. Whether he is a liberal or a conservative, he has had not one, but two educations. With a conscience acquired in childhood, he has to live as a grownup—and as a parent—in a business society which presses him unceasingly to betray that conscience. However—despite the agonizing split between our two American societies—not many Americans make the kind of spectacular bargain with evil that Faust made. Fallible most of us are, but not as a rule *that* fallible.

What usually happens is that, under the merciless crowding of the business society—sometimes also known as "progress"—the mid-century American surrenders his ethical birthright in little bits and pieces. A point yielded here. Something left unsaid there. We try to "adjust," as the psychologists say, to a situation where no adjustment is possible. And we do not usually find out—until it is too late, until too much has been given up—what has happened to us.

American chronic anxiety can be very easily explained. The Judeo-Christian ethic is the source of all our public and private morality, and that ethic has changed very little in the past two thousand years. The American business society, on the other hand, is one of the quickest-moving, most swiftly-developing and fastest-evolving of all human societies. Consequently, the faster the business society moves—the more real privacy gives way to the false intimacy of nation-wide publicity—the more money flows to the top, while the human beings (*all* human beings) sink to the bottom—the more barrenly impersonal and aimlessly mechanized our lives become—the more these things happen, the more the American people are faced with a truly grisly situation. That situation is just this: The American business society must either stop "progressing," or it must find some way of scuttling and getting rid of the money-rejecting Western ethic.

And this last is exactly what—since the end of World War II—American business has been trying to bring about. No deliberate evil-doing is involved. It is strictly a matter of "Father, forgive them, for they know not what they do." Not villainy, but social training is the point at issue. When human beings are educated and conditioned as a certain number of Americans are educated and conditioned by the business society, those human beings will continue automatically to act out that conditioning until the Grim Reaper stops the process. Unless, of course, the people who have been less strongly conditioned are able and willing to put the brake on.

The American business society is currently self-hypnotized. It has persuaded itself that in celebrating the importance of money and the superiority of the money-making personality, it is fighting Communism. What the business society is actually doing is engaging in a compulsive attempt to destroy our traditional national morality. That is why American parents have tightened nerves. In the United States, there is no way of having a good parent-child relationship except against the background of a generally acknowledged and generally practiced system of ethics. But the Hiss trials illumined with dreadful clarity what is really taking place upon our native heath.

The enormous amount of attention given by the newspapers to the Hiss trials is a fairly clear indication that something much more significant was involved than a mere technical adjudication on a perjury charge. And in reality, it was not the primary social purpose of the Hiss trials to disestablish Mr. Hiss. That was secondary. The meaning of the Hiss trials—as a social phenomenon—was that they were an unconscious attempt, on the part of the business society, to toss our official national morality overboard and to set up its own ethic instead—its own ethic being, of course, anti-Communism. In the Hiss trials, and in the person of Whittaker Chambers, the business society and the communications industry were trying to bring into general acknowledgment and good repute a kind of behavior which would have all the appearance of being an ethic—but which would not raise any awkward questions about the money-changers in the Temple.

But it is impossible to make an ethic out of anti-Communism. To be sure, there are countries in the world where it takes superlative courage to be an anti-Communist. But the United States is not one of them. An ethic implies discipline and effort. More importantly, an ethic directs people *toward* something, not merely *away from* something. Western-world morality directs people toward the good. Anti-Communism, as it is presently practiced and recognized in the United States, is a fussy, spinsterish, semi-hysterical flight from evil. But it is not, in itself, an approach to the good. To approach the good, you have to have muscles.

European observers are fond of saying that Americans are temperamentally optimistic; and personally, this writer does not deny the soft impeachment. American chronic anxiety is by no means completely incurable. That is to say, we do not have to *create* good human beings in the United States of America. We have millions and millions of them already extant. All we have to do is to stop scaring them to death—to cease spitting on their do-gooder gaberdines, and to desist from beating them over the head with the ten-cent-store morality of anti-Communism.

As Americans, all of us now mature are condemned to a certain amount of schizophrenia. (To talk about getting away from business attitudes is easy enough; but it is a long, slow process to weed them out of the habit-dominated mind.) We do not, however, have to pass on the split personality—in all its shattering completeness—to our children. There is still an Upward Step available to American parents, although that step is no longer the comparatively simple matter of earning the money for expensive schools or expensive skills.

As Americans, we have a heritage which is not only ancient and glorious, but which is also—what is more to the point—psychologically and emotionally suited to the

274

needs of warmth-seeking human beings. We do not have to invent, explore or pioneer. All we have to do is turn our backs on the cactus forest of Eggcups and put our heritage to work. There is conflict in all societies. At the very simplest, there is usually conflict between the young and the old. But no tribe or commonwealth in the world has ever demanded that people should be both young and old at the same time, the way Americans are expected to be both pious and acquisitive in one single breath. "When a society is perishing," said Pope Leo XIII, in his encyclical letter on the condition of labor, May 15, 1891, "the true advice to give to those who would restore it is to recall it to the principles from which it sprang."

A NOTE ABOUT THE AUTHOR

READERS *of this book will learn a great deal about Margaret Halsey in her own words. The publisher, therefore, is concerned only with statistics in this brief note.*

Miss Halsey was born in Yonkers, New York. She got her B.S. from Skidmore College, her M.A. from Teachers College, and then worked—in moderately rapid succession —for a bank, a real-estate company, a radio agent, and a publisher. In 1936 she married and went for a year's visit to England, during which time she wrote her first book, With Malice Toward Some. *Since then she has written* Some of My Best Friends Are Soldiers, Color Blind, *and* The Folks at Home.